Praise for *Marathon Quest*

Marathon Quest is not only a fascinating story of Martin Parnell's incredible journey to improve the lives of children the world over, but it is an exemplary illustration of what one can achieve when they put their heart and soul into something. Great book . . . amazing man!—JON MONTGOMERY, *Olympic gold medalist*

I was honored to meet and become friends with Martin on a Right To Play trip to Benin, Africa. As I got to know Martin, I was amazed to learn about his incredible endurance through 250 marathons in one year all benefiting Right To Play. His journey to change personal tragedy into a driving force to impact the lives of many children around the world is both inspiring and touching. You will cry, laugh and be deeply moved by this unbelievable book!—CAROLINE OUELLETTE, *three-time Olympic hockey medallist*

Martin proves that there is no time in life that is "too late." By stepping out and reaching for our dreams we all can be extraordinary. Martin's actions truly demonstrate a philosophy that through dedication and hard work we can achieve great things, no matter how young or old we are.—RAY ZAHAB, *adventurer, ultramarathoner and founder of impossible2Possible (i2P)*

Reading this book will having you laughing, cheering, celebrating and crying along with Martin on his remarkable journey of hope and his determined, unwavering persistence to make a difference in this world. It will also, more importantly, affirm all that you know to be good about humanity and our ability to effect change, one small step at a time.—BECKIE SCOTT, *Olympic Champion and member of the International Olympic Committee*

Martin's story in *Marathon Quest* and beyond is a heartwarming account of how one seemingly ordinary person set himself amazing physical challenges and worked tirelessly to succeed because of his commitment to a good cause. An entertaining read that will leave you inspired to be a better person, to believe anything is possible if you are dedicated enough, to think about what you too can do to help others who are less fortunate. This book is education and entertainment all rolled into one.
—ELLIE GREENWOOD, *2010 International Association of Ultrarunners 100 km World Champion and 2011 Western States Endurance Run winner*

Reading Martin's story is like closing a circle. Ten years ago I was inspired to create the definitive cycling adventure from Cairo to Cape Town, the Tour d'Afrique. One of my goals was to give something back to the people and places en route. By reading about Martin's epiphany on the tour, and how he became inspired to run 250 marathons for charity, now closes the circle and inspires me to tackle more adventures, doing some good in the process. Martin's journey is a great read and a great example of how one good action generates other.—HENRY GOLD, *founder and director of Tour d'Afrique Ltd.*

In *Marathon Quest*, Martin Parnell chronicles the inspirational athletic sojourn that led to his passionate commitment to the Right To Play movement. In its truest form—when it is fun and values-based—sport at the community level has the power to touch people's lives more profoundly than any one athlete's performance can. Right To Play leverages the high public profile of charismatic, high-achieving athletes like Martin Parnell to maximize lasting social change at home and internationally for those who can benefit the most.—BARBARA KAY, *award-winning columnist for the* National Post

Marathon Quest is an inspiring true story of how one man challenged himself, encountered major obstacles but never gave up, and in the end raised hundreds of thousands of dollars, as well as the spirits of children who need it most. What a story! — HAYLEY WICKENHEISER, *four-time Olympic hockey medalist and author of* Gold Medal Diary

For anyone who thinks the world is now all about me, me, me, Martin Parnell and his book *Marathon Quest* will change your mind instantly! To run 250 marathons in one year, through bitter cold to scorching sun, through every ache and pain imaginable, raising money for kids around the world and Right To Play is incredibly heartwarming! There are still wonderful people in this world, Martin Parnell is one of the best!—DICK BEARDSLEY, *American long distance runner and best-selling author*

His mother-in-law dubbed him the "Brit with Grit," but as his original vision has since come to fruition and he is now into chasing a Guinness World Record for a very worthy cause, Martin Parnell is also deserving of being referred to as the "Ultimate Ultra Quester." As he "enjoys" the journey, readers will thoroughly enjoy this book.—STEVE KING, *World Triathlon Champion, and commentator for* CBC, TSN, CTV *and* ESPN

Marathon Quest sheds light on how an individual can change the world one step at a time.—BART YASSO, *Chief Running Officer for Runners' World*

You will be awe inspired to read the story of Martin who, at 55, committed to run 250 marathons in one year. Martin took on this challenge not just for the many physical and mental gifts it bestowed on him, but for his passion to support an international humanitarian organization, Right To Play.—JOHN STANTON, *owner of The Running Room and best-selling author*

Martin gives an unflinchingly honest account of how he began running as an escape from grief and how that turned into an obsession he's used to raise hundreds of thousands of dollars for charity. I don't know how anyone could run 250 marathons a year, let alone in Cochrane, Alberta, where the winter temperatures dip to –30 and the summers are equally extreme. But Martin does it and takes us along for the journey. His story is written with clarity and humour, sharing intimate details that parachute us into the world of extreme marathon running and fundraising. It inspires and delights, and proves just how much of a difference one person with a dream can make, especially if he has grit and a limitless ability to endure pain.—JULIE ANGUS, *adventurer and best-selling author*

RUNNING TO THE EDGE

MARTIN PARNELL

RMB

To Hugh,

Start slow, finish fast,

Best wishes,

Martin Parnell

RMB | Rocky Mountain Books Ltd.
rmbooks.com
@rmbooks
facebook.com/rmbooks

Cataloguing data available from Library and Archives Canada

ISBN 978-1-77160-172-6 (paperback)
ISBN 978-1-77160-173-3 (electronic)

Cover photo by Chris Bolin Photography Inc.

Printed and bound in Canada by Friesens

Distributed in Canada by Heritage Group Distribution and in the U.S. by Publishers Group West

For information on purchasing bulk quantities of this book, or to obtain media excerpts or invite the author to speak at an event, please visit rmbooks. com and select the "Contact Us" tab.

RMB | Rocky Mountain Books is dedicated to the environment and committed to reducing the destruction of old-growth forests. Our books are produced with respect for the future and consideration for the past.

We acknowledge the financial support of the Government of Canada through the Canada Book Fund and the Canada Council for the Arts, and of the province of British Columbia through the British Columbia Arts Council and the Book Publishing Tax Credit.

To everyone who has supported me and,

consequently, changed the lives of thousands

of children, giving them the right to play.

———————————

"Quest: A long search for something
that is difficult to find, or an attempt to
achieve something difficult."
– *Cambridge English Dictionary*

"Play is often talked about as if it were a relief from
serious learning. But, for children, play is serious
learning. Play is really the work of children."
– FRED ROGERS, minister, TV presenter, author
of *The World According to Mr. Rogers*

Contents

Foreword

In the fall of 2014, whilst compiling the manuscript for this book, Martin's thoughts turned to whom he might approach to write the foreword. He shared his thoughts with me, names ranging from Olympic gold medalist Clara Hughes and Olympian and TV presenter Jon Montgomery, to the recipient of the 2014 World Mayor Prize, Calgary's very own Naheed Nenshi.

Fast forward to July 2015. Martin and I were on one of his daily 8-kilometre "walks to recovery" that were helping him keep fit and combat the frustrations of being able to do little else, due to the life-threatening blood clot that had had the audacity to take up residence in his brain.

As we approached the black trestle bridge that spans the Bow River 1 kilometre from our home, Martin turned to me and said, "I've been thinking…"

Now, there's something about that phrase when it's spoken by Martin that sets off alarm bells in my head. Not the loud peals one might hear emanating from a church after a wedding, or another joyous occasion, but more like those little tinkling sleigh bells that foretell of things to come. Only, in my case, the sound of those bells doesn't conjure up images of treats under a tree but rather hours, days or even weeks of worry and disruption.

I thought back to some of the more memorable events that have followed those words, "I've been thinking…of running a marathon a day for one year," "…of climbing Mount Kilimanjaro in 24 hours," "…of running 1000 kilometres of the South West Coast Path of England in a month," or "…of driving across Canada and attempting to set ten Guinness World Records along the way."

From the first time I trudged across a muddy field, at 2 a.m., carrying water, sandwiches, bananas and clean socks to an aid station in the middle of nowhere during his first ultramarathon, I knew life with Martin was going to be different.

Wives and girlfriends have often asked me how I put up with Martin's feats, and one good friend said, "You didn't sign up for this. Did you?"

To be honest, there have been times when I've wondered why I've supported him through the past five years, considering the sacrifices we've both had to make in order for him to pursue his goals. There have been times when I've asked myself if it's all been worth it. But the answer is always the same. It's absolutely been worth it because he has done it all for a cause. Every event has been a fundraiser for the humanitarian organization Right To Play and, by raising funds for RTP, Martin has improved the lives of thousands of the world's most disadvantaged children and helped them gain life skills that will be passed on for generations to come.

Martin has a quiet determination that has seen him endure and overcome many obstacles. He has inspired countless people to take on challenges and improve the lives of themselves and others. He is a role model to our children and grandchildren, who love him dearly.

I am proud to be known as Martin Parnell's wife.

Oh, and the thing that he'd been thinking about, on the way to the trestle bridge? That I should write the foreword to this book.

Now that really was a crazy idea!

– Sue Carpenter-Parnell, 2016

Preface

"Challenges make you discover things about yourself
that you never really knew."

– CICELY TYSON, actress and author of *The River Niger*

3 a.m., Friday, February 27, 2015

I open my eyes and everything is a blur. I find myself lying in a
bed. All I can hear is beep, beep, beep. I realize it's coming from a
machine, to the left of me. The room is filled with shadow and light. I
make out the red lettering of an exit sign above the door, and there's
a flickering, florescent light in the corridor, outside. I look down at
my left arm, and I see two of them; I see two of everything. Two lines
are hooked up from two IV bags into my two left arms. My head is
pounding, and I need it to stop. I call out, but nobody hears. I fumble
around and find a call button, resting on top of the bedclothes. I

press it and two white shapes enter the room. A female voice asks me, "How is the pain, out of ten?" I say ten. She says she will give me some morphine, and I thank her.

I lie still and the pain begins to ease. I close my eyes. I ask myself questions. What am I doing in this hospital room? Where is the hospital? How did I get here? And, most important, what is wrong with me?

This was not the plan. As I lay there, I began searching my memory for what might have happened. I had left Calgary 48 hours earlier to attend the Recreation Connections Manitoba Conference in Winnipeg. I had been engaged to give a keynote speech and workshop: Ordinary to Extraordinary. For the past few days, I had been taking medication for what I thought was a migraine. I then remembered that, on arriving at the conference hotel early Wednesday morning, my "migraine" had worsened, and I was nauseous.

As my symptoms deteriorated, the event organizer, Susanne, insisted I let her assistant, Cory, drive me to Grace Hospital Emergency. After receiving medication through an IV and undergoing a precautionary CT scan, I had returned to the hotel. But I was soon back at the hospital, where I was transferred to the Health Sciences Centre and put into an induced coma. When I woke, a specialist informed me that a cerebral venous sinus thrombosis, an extensive and life-threatening blood clot, had formed in the superior sagittal sinus, right transverse sinus and into the jugular vein. The hospital had notified Sue, and she was on her way. As I drifted back into a drug-induced sleep, I remember thinking, "Is this it?"

Over the last six years I had chosen to take on a number of extreme physical challenges and travelled the world to raise money for the humanitarian organization Right To Play, with the aim of changing the lives of thousands of children. But now I was facing the biggest challenge of my life, and it had chosen me.

ONE

Mine's a Guinness

"A day without sunshine is like, you know, night."
— STEVE MARTIN, comedian and author of *Born Standing Up*

In 2010 I ran 250 marathons in one year, raised $322,000 for the humanitarian organization Right To Play and gave the gift of hope to 6,440 children. That was it. I had done my bit. Then I received an invitation from Right To Play to visit a number of schools in Benin, West Africa. Seeing the work RTP was doing with the children was transformative, and on the flight back to Calgary, an idea formed: to attempt ten quests in five years, raise $1 million for Right To Play and help 20,000 children. Quests for Kids was born. Marathon Quest 250 was the first quest, and I pondered what the second one would be. In April 2011 I played an exhibition game of netball, and started to have discussions with Netball Alberta about attempting a Guinness World Record (GWR) for the *longest netball game. This was a massive undertaking, and stress quickly built as the event drew nearer. To pull this off, the players had to play 61 hours and the whole thing had to be filmed and documented. This would be Quest #2 – Netball Quest 61.*

On the morning of December 25, 1965, I received one of my favourite Christmas presents ever, a copy of the *Guinness Book of World Records* (*GBofWR*). Some of my school friends had already dipped into this book and had told me how amazing it was. The book had a shiny cover with glossy pages filled with incredible pictures and facts. Flipping through the book, I read about the oldest man, the woman with the longest fingernails, the tallest building, the strangest creatures and the fastest humans on Earth. Needless to say, I was engrossed.

In early 2011, 45 years after I had been given my first copy, I purchased my second one. I was interested to see if the 250 marathons I had run, in 2010, might qualify as a record. However, after contacting Guinness, I was told that the record is 105 race marathons, held by Larry Mecon of the U.S. Despite the fact that all 250 of my marathons had been verified, only a few of them were official races, so I didn't meet Guinness's criteria. My conversation with the folks at Guinness got me thinking about other records I might attempt and eventually led me to Quests for Kids. These quests would all consist of sports children could, potentially, take part in at school, in their local communities or at home. I wanted each quest to be an attempt at a Guinness World Record. My intention was that each event might encourage children to be active and act as fundraisers for Right To Play. I thought a long game of netball might make a good start.

By early September, I had begun to feel sick. The pressure of organizing Netball Quest 61 was beginning to build. We only had two weeks to go, and there was still a ton of stuff we needed to sort out. So far we had 19 of the 24 players – not bad, but we still needed another five. I also had to find two of the official timing devices that Guinness required but had had no luck thus far. The cost of hiring the South Fish Creek Recreational Complex, where the event would be held, was $5,000, and the videography would be $4,000, but we'd raised only $1,000. Julie Arnold from Netball Alberta was pushing to get volunteers, and we still needed food suppliers to donate meals. Julie really was the glue holding all the little pieces together. Another bright, calm spot in this tense landscape was Pablo. He was with Radio Canada International and wanted to set up a web page that would detail information on all of the Quests for Kids events, including this one.

I decided to go for a run. But first I stopped at Guy's Café in Cochrane, where I saw the usual suspects from the Red Rock Running Club: Frank, Sue, Pam, Chad, Dan, Karen, John and my friend Lau. The previous week, I had asked the club's president, Gerry, to forward an email to all members, asking for help with the quest. I was looking for two players and as many volunteers as I could muster. Unfortunately, I hadn't heard a thing back from anyone.

Chad asked me how it was going, and I let it all out. He could tell I was at my wits' end. He said he would put the word out to the 1,800 members of the Co-op Whole Health Challenge, which encouraged families to follow a healthy diet for three months and write about their experiences. Chad also offered to contact his friend Jackie, who ran an event company, to see what she could do. Kevin, the Brit who works for Calgary Police Services, jumped in. He said he knew several crazy cops who might just be tempted to engage in 61 hours of netball. These displays of enthusiasm for my cause brought me some temporary relief.

Before leaving, I chatted with my friend Frank, whose wife Liz plays in the Cochrane pipe band. I told him it would be great if the teams could be piped into the gym on September 16. Most members of the band were heading over to Beijing and wouldn't be able to play. Only one member was staying, Susan Flowers. I knew Susan, and I called her later that week.

I was feeling a little better about the quest. As I ran home along the river trail, my cell phone rang. It was Julie. She had talked to the Netball Alberta executive group, which was willing to cover the facility fee if we couldn't get the money together in time. She was also, slowly, reducing the cost of the videography. She'd already whittled it down from $19,000 to $4,000, and she thought she might be able to get the cost down even more. Julie also mentioned that the posters and flyers were ready. I figured we were getting there, after all.

On the morning of Saturday, September 10, I finally met all 24 members of the Netball Quest 61 squad. Julie had found the final five players from her Senior B league, and here we all were at 11 a.m., ready for our first and final practice session.

Up until that point, I had only met four of the team members, so I took some time that morning to learn about everyone else. After reading each of the players' biographies, some very interesting facts emerged.

1. Eight team members were male (Buzz Bishop, Scott Cable, Pete

Estabrooks, Lau Mafuru, Marc Morin, me, Jai Pravitesh Narayan and Chris Rodda) and 16 were female (Megan-Lee Aldwinckle, Sarah Badr, Aleasha Bremner, Caroline Csak, Sarah Courtney, Clarissa Given, Madison Milne-Ives, Waireka Morris, Pamela Reid, Andrea Seel, Christina Smith, Lindsey Stephen, Aimee Tannahill, Janine Tannahill, Danielle Williams and Emma Wilton).

2. Twelve were Senior A players, five were Senior B and seven had very little netball experience (to be kind).
3. Team member birthplaces included Australia, Canada, England, Fiji, New Zealand, South Africa and Tanzania.
4. A number of the players had represented Canada at the international level in netball.
5. Several players were elite athletes in various sports, including lacrosse (Scott Cable) and bobsleigh (Olympian Christina Smith).
6. Pete Estabrooks is one of Canada's pre-eminent fitness trainers.
7. Buzz Bishop is a social media guru.

During our practice, we bonded and worked out the kinks. Julie continued to keep the organizational balls in the air. The logistics were mind-boggling. Making our game a GWR event meant there had to be hundreds of checks and counter checks. Julie had lined up over 70 volunteers to be umpires, timekeepers and witnesses. The videographer was ready to get 61 hours of netball on tape – and Guinness also wanted a one-hour DVD including all the "highlights."

After our practice, I felt that we could do it. The team members parted ways – but we would meet again soon, on Friday, September 16, when we would all arrive back at the recreation centre, this time with our sleeping bags and toothbrushes, when, at 5:30 p.m., the record-breaking attempt would begin.

Guinness Book of World Records

On May 4, 1951, Sir Hugh Beaver, then the managing director of Guinness Breweries, joined a shooting party in County Wexford, Ireland. He and a fellow hunter argued over which was the fastest game bird in Europe: the koshin golden plover or the grouse. At the time, it was impossible to prove either case, as Beaver found out when he could not find this data in the reference books of the time.

Beaver knew that there must be numerous other questions, debated nightly, in pubs throughout Ireland and Britain, but no book existed to supply the answers. He realized that such a book might be popular. He discussed the idea with his friend Christopher Chataway, who contacted twin brothers Norris and Ross McWhirter. They were then running a fact-finding agency in London. In August 1954 the brothers were commissioned to put together what would become *The Guinness Book of World Records.* The first edition enjoyed a print run of 1,000, and copies were given away. Since then, the popular book has gone on to hold a world record of its own: the best-selling, copyrighted book series of all time.

The big day arrived and Sue and I made our way to the centre, hoping that all would go according to plan. I carried a large bag containing all my sports kit, sleeping bag and spares of just about everything.

Julie arrived with the players' schedule. She hadn't slept for two nights and was running on fumes. This undertaking had proven far greater than either of us had ever envisioned. Everything had come down to the last minute. Even figuring out the rotation schedule for the players had proven a huge challenge. Just three days before, I had managed to track down the official timing devices, but I hadn't had a chance to test them. They belong to Bruce Robin, a timer for Athletics

Canada, who, as it turned out, only lived two blocks down from me in Cochrane.

We were scheduled to start playing at 5:30 p.m., but at 5:40 we were still taping the court, counting players and setting up the video camera. At 5:57 Susan Flowers led the players out, playing her bagpipes. There was one heart-stopping moment when, at precisely 6:00 p.m., the referee blew the start whistle, I pressed the buttons on the timing machines and nothing happened. I pressed them again and held my breath. This time the seconds started ticking away, and I could breathe again.

The two teams were named The Rockers and the Rollers. Julie had scheduled each player to play for eight hours and then rest for four until the 61 hours was completed. The aim was to make the most of the rest periods: to shower, eat and get some sleep.

The sleeping area was at the back of the gym, separated from the court by a curtain. We made the most of a pile of crash mats. Shifts came and went, blisters were lanced and twisted ankles were taped. Some people couldn't sleep and others overslept and had to be shaken awake.

As we approached the 60-hour mark, I went over to check the timing machines and was shocked to find that instead of reading 59 hours and 58 minutes, they read 28 hours and 58 minutes. Knowing how specific Guinness is about the way in which the time has to be recorded, Julie and I were freaking out, but there was nothing we could do. We just had to go with our hand timers and continue to keep track with them.

After 60 hours of play, we had equalled the previous record. Then, at last, on Monday, September 19, at 7 a.m., we hit 61 hours, and everyone went nuts, cheering so loudly we thought the roof might well come down. Pending verification, a new Guinness World Record was set and all the sleep deprivation, exhaustion and injuries were forgotten. We were all on a high, and after the obligatory media interviews, we headed home to rest our weary limbs.

Trying to achieve a Guinness World Record in an endurance event has two major challenges: one, having the endurance to complete the task, and, two, making sure that all requirements set down by Guinness are met (and there are many). After Netball 61 finished, Julie and I sat down to put together the package of evidence, confirming the success of our attempt. Julie contacted the videographer for the 61 hours of footage, and we were in for another shock. She was told that the first 12 minutes were missing. We had no idea how, but there was nothing we could do.

We had all our witness statements and timing sheets signed by our volunteer timers, many photographs and a DVD of the highlights of the event.

I contacted Bruce with regards to the hiccup we experienced with the timing machines, and he explained that the units could only record a maximum of 32 hours at a time. When I checked them at the 60-hour mark, the machines had already tripped over and started again. He said he'd write a letter to Guinness, explaining what had happened. After many hours of checking and re checking, filling in forms and gathering documentation, on October 24, with fingers crossed, we mailed our package off to London. Now it was just a matter of waiting to see if Guinness would confirm our new record. We would wait for two long months.

Unfortunately, the euphoria of achieving a Guinness World

Record was quickly crushed by some tragic news. On that same Monday morning, I pulled into our driveway and saw Sue waiting for me in the garage. I only had to look at her face to know that something terrible had happened, and I had a feeling the news would be about my sister, Janette. I came down to Earth with a bang.

Sue held me close and explained that she'd just got a call from my brother Peter: Jan had passed away in the night. She had been sick for some time after having been diagnosed with cancer of the esophagus. The end came fairly quickly, and we can only be grateful that she didn't suffer for long.

Janette and I had been close since Mum and Dad sent her over to Canada in the spring of 1979; she was 20 and I was 24. I had been living in Kimberley, BC, for two years and was working as a mining engineer at the Sullivan Mine. Jan was a bit of a rebel, and Mum and Dad thought that six months with her older brother might do her good.

Over the next few months we explored the area around Kimberley, including going to the hot springs at White Swan. Jan loved her time in the mountains, and toward the end of her stay, we decided to go on an adventure: an eight-day camping/canoeing expedition in northern BC, at Bowron Lakes.

We canoed, fished, cooked and camped. On the seventh day, we ran out of food and Jan begged a meal from a group of Cub Scouts, who were on an adventure of their own. We survived the trip, and Jan went back to England. We stayed in touch over the years, but it wasn't until after my first wife, Wendy, died of cancer in 2001 that I really reconnected with her again.

In the fall of 2003, my children Kyle and Kristina had left home and I had quit my job. I felt a strong need to return to England and see Jan and the rest of my family. I asked Jan and her husband Austin if I could stay with them for awhile, and they said yes. In our correspondence before my departure, Jan mentioned that she had a friend, Sue, who she wanted me to meet.

I arrived in Bournemouth, on the south coast of Dorset, in late November and immediately became part of Jan and Austin's social circle. Christmas came and went, and Jan told me that we would be spending New Year's Eve with their friends Julie and Bob. That would be just before I headed up to London, to see my sister Sally and then return to Canada. On New Year's Eve, we headed over to Julie and Bob's. I walked into their kitchen and was introduced to Sue. We hit it off straight away, and when we got to the restaurant I made sure I sat next to her. We were at an Italian place called La Mamma's and Sue and I chatted and danced all evening.

I felt so at ease in her company, as if I'd known her a long time. The next day, Sue phoned to see if I would like to meet for supper before I headed up to London. I said yes, and the rest, as they say, is history.

I didn't see Jan again until 2011. Sue and I were visiting England. By this time, Jan had gone through numerous sessions of chemotherapy and was putting up a very brave fight against the cancer that was rampaging through her body. We spent a wonderful afternoon with her, walking along the beach near Bournemouth, toward Boscombe Pier. We ate ice cream and checked out the renovated beach huts along the sea front. Despite everything she was going through, as always, she looked fantastic. She was so full of life, exactly how Sue and I want to remember her.

In early September, my brother Peter received a call that Jan had been moved to a hospice. Pete and I booked our flights and planned to head out on September 21 to spend some time with her, but, sadly, Pete and I were now heading over for her funeral.

I sat in the crematorium alongside Peter, my other brother Andrew, and sisters Sally and Louise. The celebration of life service reflected how Janny had lived her life. She had chosen the music herself, from the opening Tom Waits song, "Jockey Full of Bourbon," to "Can't Take My Eyes Off of You," by Lauryn Hill, dedicated to her husband, Austin. I'll always think of Jan with love for her amazing spirit, and with endless gratitude for bringing Sue and me together.

Quest #2: By the Numbers

Netball Quest 61 (September 16 –19, 2011)
Objective: To play 61 hours of netball and set a Guinness World Record
Location: South Fish Creek Recreational Complex, Calgary, Alberta, Canada
Status: Guinness World

Record set (61 hours, 00 minutes, 00 seconds)
Donations: $22,600
Matching funds: $0
Total: $22,600
Kids helped: 452
Funds application: To Right To Play's highest-priority project, unrestricted

TWO

Go East Young Man

"The journey of a thousand miles begins with one step."
—LAO TZU, *Tao Te Ching*

After Netball Quest 61 and the death of my sister, Janette, Sue and I needed a break and some time together. We decided on a road trip around the Maritimes. The journey took us to a number of out-of-the-way places in Prince Edward Island (PEI), Nova Scotia and New Brunswick. I even found a marathon to run in Charlottetown.

One of the best holidays you can take is a road trip. Throw a couple of suitcases in the trunk, buy a tank full of gas and away you go. In the past, Sue and I had travelled west to Tofino on Vancouver Island and north to Yellowknife. But now we headed to Canada's east coast for two weeks. Our plan was to tour three of the Atlantic provinces: Nova Scotia, New Brunswick and PEI.

After arriving at Halifax Stanfield International Airport, we picked up our rental car and headed into the city. The next couple of days were spent exploring the harbour and surrounding area. The highlight was a visit to Pier 21, a passenger terminal for trans-Atlantic ocean liners from 1928 until 1971. Liners docked at a long seawall wharf, divided into piers 20, 21, 22 and 23. Immigration facilities were located at Pier 21. It had a railway booking office and passenger train sidings for special immigration trains, as well as an overhead walk-way to the railway station. The pier was the primary point of entry for over one million immigrants and refugees from Europe and else-where, as well as the departure point for 496,000 Canadian military personnel during the Second World War. The facility became known informally as the Gateway to Canada.

Pier 21 was closed in 1971 but reopened as a museum in 1999. This museum tells the stories of the 1.5 million immigrants and Canadian troops who passed through its doors. As Sue and I went around the exhibits, we read a number of personal stories of immigrants who had tried to come to Canada. Some had made it; others were turned back. I immigrated to Canada in 1977. If I had arrived only six years earlier, I would have gone through Pier 21.

On the road, we headed 45 kilometres southwest to one of Nova Scotia's must-sees, Peggy's Cove. We arrived mid-morning and the place was deserted. Peggy's Cove is a small, picturesque fishing vil-lage with a population of 120. It's located on a narrow ocean inlet, which provides safe haven for boats during the Atlantic's rough weather. The main attraction is the lighthouse. Our camera was soon in overdrive. As we made our way back to the headland, six large buses pulled into the parking lot and out poured about 400 sightseers. We asked one of the bus drivers what was going on, and he said it was cruise-ship season and these visitors were from a liner that had just arrived in Halifax from New York. Time to hit the road.

We took a three-hour trip on *The Princess of Acadia*, a ferry plying the Bay of Fundy from Digby to Saint John, New Brunswick. The Bay of Fundy has the largest tidal bore in the world at 17 metres from high tide to low tide. The crossing was relatively smooth: Sue spotted two whales and I spotted lots of seagulls.

We headed to Fredericton to visit our friends Tom and Ulrica Healy. Tom suggested he and I join up with the Capital City Runners later that afternoon. We met the group on a path near the university and headed out for a slow run. That's the great thing about running and travelling: go to any town or city and check out the local club's running schedule. They always welcome visiting runners.

I started chatting with a member named Gabriella, who works at the university and had started a Right To Play Club. She mentioned the Prince Edward Island Marathon coming up the following Sunday, in Charlottetown. It had to be fate because Sue and I had planned to be in Charlottetown for the weekend. Sue signed up for the 5-kilometre run because it went along the coastline – great for pictures.

After saying goodbye to our friends, we headed to the Hopewell Rocks, nicknamed the Flowerpots, which are on the shores of the upper reaches of the Bay of Fundy, at Hopewell Cape, near Moncton, New Brunswick. Due to the extreme tidal range of the bay, twice a day the base of the formations is covered in water. We arrived at the site at 10 a.m., fortunately at low tide, so we could view the rocks from ground level. We scrambled down a rickety wooden ladder and spent an hour exploring. Locals are trying to have the Bay of Fundy labelled one of the "Seven New Wonders of the World," and I can see why. We cast our vote at a kiosk on our way out of Hopewell Rocks park.

When planning our Maritimes road trip, I had made up a three-ring binder (I'm an engineer, after all) of the key things to do and see. A number of items had been ticked off already; now it was time to check out one of the top Canadian feats of engineering, Confederation Bridge, which connects New Brunswick to PEI. Construction took place from the autumn of 1993 to the spring of 1997; the 12.9-kilometre bridge ended up costing $1.3 billion. PEI's government is canny. It costs nothing to cross the bridge onto the island, but there's a toll to get off.

First on our PEI schedule was to head to the North Cape and see the Atlantic Wind Test Site (AWTS). By mid-October, things start to close down. In fact, that day was the interpretive centre's last day of the season.

We headed northwest and, in Tignish, found the Murphys' B & B, about 10 kilometres from the cape. Peter and Louise, originally from Ottawa, had been running the guest house for three years. We headed up to the test site before dark. The mist was coming in, and several huge windmills loomed eerily on the horizon. When we got out of the car, we were almost blown over.

The interpretive centre was still open, but it was closing in one hour, making us the last visitors of the year. The North Cape is one of the windiest places in Canada and the AWTS was established in 1980 as Canada's National Wind Energy Laboratory. Since then it has been the cornerstone of Canada's wind energy research and development program. PEI now draws more than 5 per cent of its electricity from wind energy at North Cape.

One of the reasons I wanted to stay at Tignish is that it is at the start of the Trans Canada Trail. This route, also known as the Confederation Trail, goes from one end of PEI to the other. It was developed on abandoned railway lines and travels through wetlands, hardwood groves and quaint villages and along rivers. In August 2000 PEI became the first province in Canada to complete a section of the trail. The section from Tignish to Elmira is 273 kilometres long and is promoted as a cycle route, but, with its crushed-gravel footing, access to food and drink along the route and amazing scenery, I definitely think there's potential for an ultramarathon to be run along the route. But, in the meantime, the marathon in Charlottetown would have to do.

As I'd only heard about the PEI Marathon on the Wednesday, I really hadn't had much time to think about it before signing up. At 6:45 a.m. on the Sunday, as I was waiting for the bus in Charlottetown to take me to the race start, I saw a face that I recognized. It was Vince Perdue from the Sudbury Rocks Running Club. Vince was my mentor when I started running in 2003. He coached me through my first two marathons and helped me qualify for Boston. He, too, was on a road trip and was running two marathons along the away.

The PEI Marathon is a point to point, beginning at beautiful Brackley Beach in Prince Edward Island National Park on PEI's north shore. The start line is on the west side of the Brackley Beach change facilities, and marathoners proceed east, along the Gulf Shore Parkway, toward Dalvay.

At 7:45 a.m. we piled off the bus and headed over to the start line. We were very lucky with the weather. Apparently the year before it was wet and cold, but we were standing around in a balmy 12°C with an easterly wind. As I huddled with a group in the middle of the starters, I noticed a young lad. His name was Tyler Heggie and he was 9 years old. I asked at what pace he planned to run and he said he didn't know. He told me that his dad and brother would be pacing him, and I wished him luck. At 8 a.m. the gun went off, and Tyler left me in the dust. I would not see him again on the course.

I soon got into a good rhythm, and at every aid station I'd stop and chat with the volunteers. I don't normally eat energy gels when running, but I hadn't brought my CarboPro, so I had to eat that sticky gloop. The first half of the race was along the ocean, and then we headed inland along part of the Trans Canada Trail. After 20 kilometres I knew the halfway point was coming up. As I looked up the road, the sun was directly in my eyes – all I could make out was the silhouette of a 6-metre beaver. Another runner told me that this beaver (blown-up, not real) travels to a lot of races in the Maritimes.

At the 32-kilometre mark, I heard a yell, "Martin!" Three runners, each of them dressed as Anne of Green Gables, caught up with me. One was Cathy Hopkins, with whom I'd run the Comrades marathon in South Africa, the previous May. Running is a small world. The three Annes went ahead of me, and I came in at 4 hours, 44 minutes and 17 seconds.

There's no free lunch on PEI. You leave the island either via Confederation Bridge or a ferry from Wood Islands to Caribou, Nova Scotia. Either way you pay. We took the one-hour ferry ride and started our trip into Cape Breton and along the Cabot Trail. We had been told to drive the trail anti-clockwise for a better view. This is a good idea, but Sue is not good with heights and there were times when she just closed her eyes and held her breath.

A number of the cafés and restaurants had closed for the season, but we did find the Clucking Chicken, highly recommended for its specialty grilled-cheese sandwich. There I found a leaflet for the Two Tittle B & B. The leaflet read: *"Two Tittle is located in the tiny fishing community of White Point, a short distance off the Cabot Trail in northeastern Cape Breton. This is truly where the green of the hills meets the blue of the sea and the birthplace of renowned Scottish Fiddler, Winston Scotty Fitzgerald, whose melodies were inspired by the surrounding beauty and a simple way of life."* It sounded good.

Cyril and Marguerite welcomed us, and we had a great first night at the Two Tittle. While there, Sue and I walked the trail to White Point and visited the sailors' graveyard on the peninsula, where a total of 95 bodies are buried. The large stones represent where adults are buried and the smaller ones, children. There is one large cross for the Unknown Sailor.

We continued south around the trail and enjoyed the amazing scenery. Over the next couple of days, we visited friends in Louisdale and Port Hawkesbury.

Our final day was spent in Halifax. Irwin Shipyard had just been awarded a $25 billion, 30-year contract for a number of navy ships.

As Mayor Peter Kelly stated, "It's like winning the Olympics 30 years in a row." We headed out to Crystal Crescent Beach Provincial Park, about 20 minutes from downtown. Sue and I walked the beaches and ended up on a rock outcrop, watching the crashing waves. That evening I had my final seafood chowder. My next evening meal would be an Alberta steak.

In total, we drove 3002 kilometres on our Maritimes road trip. Now that's 71 marathons, 72 if you count the one I actually ran on PEI.

Upon our return, I knew I needed to come up with ideas for my other quests. Scott Cable had been one of the players in Netball Quest 61, and we had chatted a number of times during the event. He and his brother Shawn run a company called Hotbox Lacrosse, which sells lacrosse apparel, and he said that they would be interested in working with me on a GWR for the longest game of box lacrosse. I contacted Guinness in London and found out that such a record had never been set and to do so, a minimum of 24 hours would have to be played. I told Scott that I had never played lacrosse but was so keen to learn that I had enrolled in some lacrosse training sessions.

After a number of meetings, Scott and I agreed that we would shoot for a tentative date of April 2012 for the attempt at Lacrosse Quest 24 (LQ24).

I knew that if I wanted to complete the ten quests in five years I would have to pick up the pace. I had completed two (Marathon Quest 250 and Netball Quest 61) in two years and therefore needed three in 2012. LQ24 and Soccer Quest 42 (SQ42) were taking shape, and I needed one more. My thoughts turned to my friend Jason Webb, owner of Downunder Travel. Jason had been a supporter of

Quest #2 and during the event told me about a 31-kilometre race held annually in September, the route circumnavigating the island of Rarotonga in the Pacific Cook Islands. I went to see Jason in late October and proposed running the island three times and a bit, to make up 100 kilometres, and call it Cook Islands Quest 100. He went for it, and my third quest was born.

What a difference a year makes. Early Saturday morning, on December 31, 2011, I looked out the front door and read –5°C on the thermometer, a much more civilized temperature than it had been in

New Year's Eve

One traditional way of celebrating New Year's Eve is First Footing. Rooted in Scottish and northern English folklore, this tradition marks the first day of the New Year and sets the tone for the year ahead. The first person to cross a home's threshold on New Year's Day is, hopefully, the bringer of good fortune for the coming year. Traditionally, the First Foot is a dark-haired male. A resident of the house is also acceptable, so long as he or she is not in the house on the stroke of midnight. The First Foot is expected to bring gifts, which should include a coin, a piece of bread, some salt, a piece of coal and a drink (usually whisky). These represent, respectively, financial prosperity, food, flavour, warmth and good cheer. In Scotland this tradition is often accompanied by some form of entertainment. Sue's parents still hold with this practice. Her mum still has a piece of coal from the 1950s when her home was heated by a coal fire. She makes Sue's dad leave the house before midnight on December 31, walk around the block and then re-enter the house, ensuring that he is the First Foot. It doesn't seem to matter to them that although his hair was once jet black, it is now snowy white!

2010, when I was finishing my year of marathons. My friend David Houghton was visiting from Toronto, and we headed down to the Spray Lake Sawmills Family Sports Centre for the annual walk/run I instituted at the end of Marathon Quest 250.

A couple of days earlier I had walked the loop with Brian, one of the centre's maintenance personnel. I was a bit shocked by the condition of the trail from the facility to the pathway. With the warm weather, most of the snow was gone and large rocks were sticking up everywhere. Brian and I looked for another access and found one by a nearby campground. That day I ran the route and found that it was 2 kilometres rather than 2.5 kilometres. No problem. Participants would simply have to do 21 laps instead of 17.

On the day of the walk/run, we arrived at the centre at 8 a.m. and were met by Steve Hung, Ginelle Polini and Kimberley Quach from the University of Calgary Right To Play Club. In 2010 and 2011 they had helped out at a number of my events. Slowly, runners started to arrive, and by 8:50 we had 20 individuals ready to run the marathon. At 9 a.m. I blew my bear whistle and off we went. We completed loop after loop, and at 10 kilometres we took a break and enjoyed the hot chocolate and cookies provided by Guy's Bakery at the Super Aid Station set up in the centre's entrance.

We finished the half-marathon at 11:35 a.m. and relaxed for a few minutes. Jason Webb from Downunder Travel had set up a booth promoting the Cook Islands Quest 100. We hoped to take a group with us to Rarotonga in September 2012. Tyson Farrish and his mom Brenda; Monica Zurowski, managing editor of the *Calgary Herald*, and her friend Alison Goodchild; and Val Avery and Howard Rattai had read about the race and immediately signed up.

Throughout the day, runners joined us for the 10-, 5- and 2.5-kilometre runs, and at 3 p.m. the marathon was complete. In total we had 107 participants and raised $2,827. This would allow 140 kids to participate in a Right To Play program for one year. Right To Play would direct the funds we raised to the program with the highest need.

A Word about Right To Play

Right To Play began as Olympic Aid in 1994, the brainchild of the Lillehammer Olympic Organizing Committee (LOOC). The organization was to focus on supporting people in war-torn countries, with Olympic athletes working as ambassadors to help with fundraising. The lead Athlete Ambassador was Norwegian speed skater Johann Olav Koss, who donated a great deal of his Olympic winnings to Olympic Aid and challenged others to do the same. As a result of Koss's generosity, Olympic Aid raised $18 million, which funded five projects in 1994, including a hospital in Sarajevo, schools in Eritrea and a mother-child program in Guatemala.

The organization continued to raise money for children in dire situations between 1994 and 2000. Projects included a joint venture with UNICEF, which funnelled $13 million into a vaccination program that benefitted 12.2 million kids and more than 800,000 women. The effort resulted in temporary "Olympic Truces" in Afghanistan and the Kurdish region in northern Iraq, where fighting ceased to allow UNICEF staff to immunize the women and children.

By late 2000, Olympic Aid incorporated and became Right To Play, no longer a "fundraising vehicle" but a nongovernmental organization (NGO). Beginning in March 2001, Right To Play started implementing sport and play programs, the first ones in refugee communities in Angola and Côte d'Ivoire.

As Right To Play found its legs, it began hosting round-tables about sport relative to development issues like HIV and AIDS prevention, health and refugee rehabilitation. These roundtables have been attended by the likes of then–UN Secretary-General Kofi Annan, Archbishop Desmond Tutu, Dr. Jacques Rogge, Steven Lewis and others, who helped place sport and development on the international agenda.

Today Right To Play maintains its position as a leader in the field of sport for development. It advocates for every child's right to play and is active in trying to turn that right into a reality for kids the world over. Right To Play is working to "engage leaders on all sides of sport, business and media to ensure every child's right to play." The organization's motto is: Look After Yourself, Look After One Another.

Right To Play's programs are about playing, but there's a method to the play. Right To Play's goal in delivering sport programs to kids is to effect positive behavioural change, which involves kids acquiring the knowledge and attitudes they need to gain and maintain self-esteem, peaceful conflict-resolution skills, problem-solving skills, communication techniques and resistance to peer pressure. Right To Play recognizes that in order to support kids on their journey to acquiring these skills, someone must be there to create and maintain supportive environments, help the kids develop life skills, help the kids adopt healthy attitudes and guide them toward acquiring knowledge about local and world issues. Once established in a community, Right To Play encourages that supportive environment by enlisting the help of volunteer community members to be role models and supporters of change. Trained by Right To Play, these individuals become the Right To Play Coaches, who lead day-to-day activities. The organization then sets to work in helping kids and communities change, through programs of repetitive sport and play, guiding them from kids who *are unaware* of their ability to be community advocates to kids who *are* community advocates.

Right To Play customizes its programming based on community needs, providing games and programs that are relevant. And the results are fantastic!

THREE

Canada's National Sport

"I thought lacrosse was what you find in la church."

—ROBIN WILLIAMS, comedian

Scott Cable was keen to help organize the GWR event for the longest game of box lacrosse. The only problem was that I had never played the game. I completed a week-long boot camp at Springbank Community High School and got tips from Geoff Snider, face-off man for the Calgary Roughnecks. Lacrosse Quest 24 was ready to go.

On January 3, 2012, I received an email from Guinness World Records.

> Dear Mr. Martin Parnell,
> We are pleased to confirm that you have successfully set

the new Guinness World Records title for 'Longest marathon playing netball'.

Guinness World Records congratulates you on your achievement. Enclosed is your official Guinness World Records certificate confirming your title.

Details of your achievement have been entered into our Records Database as follows: "The longest marathon playing netball lasted 61 hours and was achieved by Netball Alberta (Canada) at the South Fish Creek Recreation Complex in Calgary, Alberta, Canada, from 16–19 September 2011."

We are pleased to welcome you to the very select club of Guinness World Records title holders.

Yours sincerely,

Manu Gautam

Guinness World Records

We had our world record. The news hit Facebook, and word travelled fast. All the participants were delighted that the hard work had paid off and were proud to know they'd soon be receiving their official certificates.

On February 18, in anticipation of the next quest, Sue and I went to our first ever lacrosse game, at the Calgary Saddledome. The Calgary Roughnecks were playing the Edmonton Rush. We watched the game with Scott, the mastermind behind LQ24. What a night. The Calgary Saddledome was packed with kids and parents. At $20 a ticket, lacrosse is a much more affordable option for families than hockey. Before the game, the crowd was entertained by the Roughnecks' mascot, the Honey Badger. Then the lights were turned off and

Traditional Lacrosse

Modern-day lacrosse descends from and is still similar to games played by First Nations and Native American communities. Games like *dehuntshigwa'es* (Onondaga), meaning "men hit a rounded object," and *da-nah-wah'uwsdi* (Eastern Cherokee), meaning "little war," and *baaga`adowe* (Ojibwe), meaning "bump hips." It's one of the oldest team sports in North America, with one of the oldest versions of lacrosse having emerged in the 17th century.

Traditional lacrosse games could last for several days. Between a hundred and a thousand men from opposing communities would play on open fields between the communities, with the goals located between 460 metres and several kilometres apart.

There was no out-of-bounds, and players could not touch the "ball" with their hands. The goals were often delineated by rocks or trees, latterly, wooden posts were pounded in. Participants would play from dawn until dusk.

A lacrosse game began with the ball being tossed into the air and the two sides rushing to catch it. Because there were so many players, the game tended to devolve into a mob swarming the ball and moving it thus across the field. For this reason, play was slow!

The medicine men acted as coaches, and women usually were on the sidelines, serving refreshments to the players. A women's version of the game was also played in some communities. The female players used shorter sticks that had larger heads.

Lacrosse traditionally had many different purposes. Some games were played to settle inter-tribal disputes. The game actually helped keep the Six Nations of the Iroquois together. Lacrosse also was a kind of training ground for young warriors learning combat; it was recreation, as part of festivals, and for the bets involved. Finally, lacrosse was played for religious reasons, to entertain the Creator, with both players and audience taking part in a collective prayer.

the Calgary players ran out under a flaming oil derrick. Throughout the game the music was relentless and the play was frenetic. The kids jumped up and down every time Calgary scored, and by the final whistle, Calgary had beat Edmonton 12–8. What a blast.

By the end of February, the National Lacrosse League (NLL) and the Professional Lacrosse Players' Association (PLPA) had announced Right To Play as their official designated joint charity. Several NLL players who have become Athlete Ambassadors for Right To Play, including Dan Dawson, Tracey Kelusky, Chris McElroy and Andrew McBride, joined Right To Play and league representatives to make the announcement. The organizations pledged to work together to design and develop a Lacrosse for Development program for kids in Ontario, in addition to helping raise $10,000 for the humanitarian organization. They seemed pretty pumped about it. And so was I.

I knew that Right To Play's Promoting Life-skills in Aboriginal Youth (PLAY) initiative would benefit a lot from the new Lacrosse for Development program. Throughout First Nations communities in Ontario, NLL players would be helping to deliver skill-based instruction to children, youth and coaches. The program continues to inspire and motivate First Nations children and youth to connect with lacrosse's culture and traditions – in many cases these traditions are also their own by birthright.

Even as I was hearing that RTP and the National Lacrosse League were building a partnership, I also received some great news from Sarah Stern, at Right To Play. The federal Department of Foreign Affairs, Trade and Development (DFATD) would be matching funds to the quests I was planning to attempt over the next two years. For every $1 raised in 2012 and 2013, DFATD would donate $3. The coun-

Promoting Life-skills in Aboriginal Youth (PLAY)

In June 2010, Right To Play, with generous funding from the Ontario Ministry of Aboriginal Affairs and partners, started up the Promoting Life-skills in Aboriginal Youth (PLAY) program, in partnership with Moose Cree and Sandy Lake First Nations. The objective of the PLAY program is to build on the strengths of Aboriginal youth and their communities, while supporting cultures and individual identities. PLAY programs are designed in partnership with individual communities and so are tailored to communities' specific needs. Before PLAY enters a community, community members participate in a needs assessment that guides the design of the program. It aims to support children and youth to develop and strengthen essential life skills. In just three years, PLAY expanded from two to 57 First Nations communities and urban Aboriginal organizations in Ontario and Manitoba, engaging over 3,300 children and youth.

As of this writing, the PLAY program reaches more than 90 First Nations communities and Aboriginal organizations in Alberta, British Columbia, Manitoba and Ontario – 3,847 kids participated in PLAY programs between 2014 and 2015. As one PLAY Community Mentor said, "The PLAY program has helped youth in my community to gain confidence and pride in being Aboriginal youth."

No matter where the program is located in the world, Right To Play uses the transformative power of sport and play to build essential life skills in children, thereby driving social change in communities affected by war, poverty and disease. So it was only natural for RTP to take up a partnership with the National Lacrosse League (NLL) relative to its PLAY program in Canada. As Robert Witchel, former national director of Right To Play Canada, said, "The NLL players driving this initiative will help create positive change in the lives of the children and youth participating."

Right To Play is supported by an international roster of over 350 Athlete Ambassadors.

try RTP selected to benefit from these matching funds was Benin in West Africa. I knew this news would be a great incentive for people to donate, and the matching funds gave us a great shot at reaching our $1 million goal. This news gave me a huge energy boost as I continued to plan the quests and learn about the games involved.

My first step in learning the skills of lacrosse was to embark on a week-long lacrosse extravaganza at Springbank Community High School – their Lacrosse Boot Camp Immersion is sometimes the only way to go!

First, I needed some gear. So I headed down to Edge Sports in Cochrane. I emptied my hockey bag in front of the owner, Gord Baker, and he just shook his head. My shoulder pads were from the 1930s and my elbow pads wouldn't fit a 9-year-old. I also had to exchange my Plexiglas hockey mask for a wire one. By the time we were done, in addition to switching out my mask, Gord had kitted me out with a new set of shoulder pads, arm-slash guards, wrist protectors and lacrosse gloves. The new gear felt great. I was ready for action.

On March 5 I arrived at the school and met Katie Frauts, a physical education teacher and great supporter of Marathon Quest 250. It took me 20 minutes to get all the gear on and in the correct order, so I was glad I had arrived a bit early.

When I marched out onto the gym floor, I was a little surprised. All the Grade 10 students were wearing shorts and T-shirts. No shoulder pads, elbow pads or kidney guards. It took me another ten minutes to remove the gear.

We started off with some warm-ups and then it was on to skills training. Katie asked Kyle, a talented player, to be my personal trainer. He showed me how to catch the ball, cradle it and shoot.

We played a game, and the kids were terrific. I went home full of enthusiasm, and Sue mused that I sounded like I used to in 2010 after coming home from running a marathon with the children at one of the local schools.

The rest of the week went by in a flash. Kyle had me shooting at targets and running passing drills. I took face-offs and played goalie. Friday came, and Jeremy from the *Cochrane Eagle* came out and took some action shots.

My lacrosse week was completed with a trip to the Saddledome to watch another Calgary vs. Edmonton game. Shawn Cable, Scott's brother, had lined up a box, and we all met at the Loungeburger before the game. My buddies Lau and Jeremy came with me. It was Lau's first time watching a game. The game was pretty even until the fourth quarter when the Roughnecks "crushed the Rush" and won 16–9.

My next step up the lacrosse training ladder was a big one. Geoff Snider of the Calgary Roughnecks offered to give me some one-on-one tuition. Geoff is a physical player who takes the face-offs for the team. He also plays for the Charlotte Hounds of Major League Lacrosse, in North Carolina, and operates Elev8 Lacrosse, which runs springtime skills camps for kids. I explained to Geoff that I was trying to set a Guinness World Record for the longest game of box lacrosse and raise money for Right To Play while doing it. Right away, he agreed to take on this old dog. After my session with Geoff on March 29, I had to soak in our hot tub – my muscles were screaming.

After that week of lacrosse immersion and Geoff's training session, I felt ready for the quest, which was set for April 27, 2012. In the meantime, however, I would engage in a variety of other activities in order to keep myself in condition. Skiing and running took up much of my time during the month of March.

I've loved skiing since I was 16, when I signed up for a one-week school trip to the French Alps with my friends Patrick and Malcolm. None of us had skied before and as there are no ski resorts in Devon, England, we decided to prepare for our trip by heading over to the Torbay Leisure Centre, which had a "dry" ski slope laid out down the side of a hill. Imagine a carpet that feels like toothbrush bristles. Every Saturday morning, for six weeks, we'd learn to snow plough and other basic skiing techniques. Things were good if you stayed vertical, but if you went down you'd get a nasty carpet burn on your elbows and knees. The best times were after a downpour, when you could fly off the end and keep going for 50 metres onto wet grass.

Fast forward to Kimberley, BC, my first home in Canada after immigrating in 1977. Besides the Happy Hans cuckoo clock, the best feature of the town is the ski hill. During my first winter, I bought a set of Lange 211 racing skis, Nordica boots and poles at a ski swap. Over the following two winters, I spent most of my free time, day and night, at the hill. My next move was to Yellowknife, NT. It's flat. No problem – I moved on to cross-country skiing.

In 1985 I moved again, this time east to Sudbury, Ontario. Again, not a mecca for downhill skiing, but our kids learned the basics at the Lively Ski Hill. We went on holiday to Searchmont (Sault Ste. Marie) and Mount St. Louis Moonstone (Barrie). In 2004, when I made my way west to Cochrane, I could head out to the big hills again. In the winter of 2006, my nephew Luke came over from England to work at the Lake Louise ski resort. He needed a Canadian Ski Instructors Alliance (CSIA) Level 1 certificate, and I joined him on the course to keep him company. We spent two weekends at Canada Olympic Park, and at the end of the program I got my certification, too.

Big-hill skiing is, in my opinion, the best. As I skied in the Rockies, musing about the coming lacrosse event, I thought back to 2011, when I had the biggest thrill I've had on the slopes, with my granddaughter Autumn in Sudbury. She was 7 years old at the time and had enrolled in the Nancy Greene learn-to-ski program. She wanted to show Papa Martin how it was done so we took the lift up to the top of the hill at Adanac Ski Centre. She took off like a bullet through the mist. We skied together until suddenly she seemed to rise into the air and disappear. I soon realized she'd gone over a jump, and in the nick of time, I swerved to the left. On the other side of the obstacle, I found Autumn in a heap. I asked if she was all right, and she just smiled, got up and kept going.

Throughout the end of that winter, even as I hit the slopes, I anticipated the coming spring and began putting my 2012 race schedule together. I was set to run the Calgary Marathon at the end of May, the Iron Legs 80-kilometre Ultra on August 11, the Cook Islands Quest 100-kilometre on September 23, and the New York Marathon on November 4. These are all great races, but on Saturday, April 14, as Lacrosse Quest loomed, I ran one of my favourites. I had been invited to lead the Co-op Toonie 2-Kilometre Race. This is the final event in the Co-op's annual Whole Health Challenge. Over a three-month period, the challenge encourages people to reflect on their diets and start exercising. The main attractions for Saturday were the 10-kilometre and 5-kilometre races, but for me, leading the kids in the Toonie 2-Kilometre was tops.

As I drove into Calgary, the snow flurries started. I arrived at

Eau Claire Mall and headed for the sign-up table. First to register was young Conner, and he planned to push the pace. A few minutes later, 3-year-old Emma signed up. Her plan was to run 500 metres – sounded good to me. At 9:50 a.m., everyone headed outside and, at 10 a.m., a large group of 10-kilometre racers headed off. The race started from the Olympic Arch and went down to the Bow River Path and westward. It was an out and back, so no tricky navigation. At 10:05 the 5-kilometre racers set off, leaving us Toonie 2-Kers to ready ourselves. I thought the race would consist of Conner and me, with Emma bringing up the rear, but at the last minute, we were joined by Emerson, Ashley and Kaylee.

At 10:20 a.m. the gun went off and we bolted from the start. Conner, Ashley and Kaylee shot off, but Emerson and I knew that a steady pace was the key. Emerson told me that she was 6 years old and in Grade 1 at Chaparral School. She had never run 2 kilometres before so this would be a new personal best for her. She was a running machine, and I had to tell her to take walk breaks. After 1.5 kilometres we caught up with Ashley and Kaylee, both in Grade 2 at the same school. We all crossed the line together in 19 minutes and 57 seconds, a very respectable time.

We were presented with our medals and stood together to have our photos taken. As we waited, I noticed the following words inscribed on the ground under the arch, "The most important thing in the Olympic Games is not to win but to take part, just as the most important thing in life is not the triumph but the struggle." Words to live by.

As I said goodbye to the kids, Emerson told me that she was off to a birthday party. Life doesn't get any better than that.

Kyle Shewfelt's Gymnastics Festival

On March 25 Sue and I drove to the Olympic Oval at the University of Calgary for a gymnastics festival produced by Kyle Shewfelt, Canadian gymnastics gold medalist. As I entered the Jack Simpson Gymnasium, I remembered the first time I had met Kyle, on August 16, 2010, just after I had run marathon #107. I had been invited to participate in one of Right To Play's main fundraisers, the Red Ball Golf Tournament at Silver Tip Golf Course, in Canmore, Alberta. In this tournament, business people sign up to play a round of golf with an Olympian. It was a miserable day, cold and wet, and I was happy to get inside and warm up.

Right To Play Canada boasts over 130 Athlete Ambassadors, who give their time to visit schools and participate in Right To Play activities. Many of these ambassadors were in the room that day. The dining room was full, but I didn't know anyone. I sat down at a table, and who should come and sit next to me but Kyle.

He introduced himself, and we hit it off right away.

Over the next year, we stayed in touch and, in September 2011, he came out to support Netball Quest 61. That year, Kyle had begun running and had completed a half-marathon. In 2012 he took on his first marathon, and I joined him on one of his long, slow, training runs. That summer he was the CTV gymnastics analyst for the London Summer Olympics. He was a busy guy, but he never dropped the ball, especially when it came to fundraising for Right To Play.

This was Kyle's second annual event. In 2011 the festival raised $10,000 for Right To Play. As Kyle noted in 2012, "At the Kyle Shewfelt Gymnastics Festival, we put a great deal of emphasis on fun. Our goal is to ensure that every participant, judge, volunteer and audience member feels like a star and has an experience they won't soon forget." Kyle lived up to his word: the event was amazing. There was action everywhere.

At last, the day of Lacrosse Quest 24 arrived. Scott and Shawn had done a fantastic job of rounding up 42 players. They had even talked four of the Netball Quest players into join the team and trying for a second GWR. A huge plus for the event was that, in late March, Julie Arnold from Netball Alberta had returned from her travels and started to help out with all the logistics required by Guinness.

At 5 p.m. on Friday, April 27, I arrived at the South Fish Creek Recreation Complex and at 7 p.m. the two teams lined up. The Donkeys consisted of Sarah Badr, Earl Blakely, Scott Cable, Keegan Davidson, Alexia Deis, Clarissa Givens, David Grant, Blaine Harwardt, David Harker, Kenny Hughes, Alex MacPherson, Ryan Mcbride, Drake Mooney, Dale Osmond, me, Josh Sartorelli, Aaron Tackaberry, Ryan Taylor, Darryl Terrio, Derek Wilson and Daniel Zentner. The opposing Unicorns included Eric Antonchuk, Ryan Avery, Brad Banister, John Berezuk, Wayne Burry, Shawn Cable, Ryan Davis, Janine Dersch, Tyler Farmer, Jacob Ferguson, Kris Handley, Tak Kyle, Matt Labarbara, Casey MacIntyre, Carmen Massel, Steve Morris, Pam Reid, Andrea Seel, Garret Stroshein, Wade Taylor and Dannica Tackaberry. The game began and, hour after hour, players rotated in and out. As each goal was scored, my friend Neil Zeller tweeted the status of the game. Bodies were laid out everywhere, each player trying to get some rest before his or her next shift. For a number of players, it was their first game, but everyone supported each other as the objective was for all of us to finish together.

At 7:02 p.m., on Saturday, April 28, the final whistle went and the game was over. There was a large crowd in the bleachers, and a huge cheer went up. Exhausted players congratulated each other. Scott and I checked the timing devices, and this time everything looked good. I collected my stuff, said goodbye to everyone and Sue drove me home. Time for some sleep.

I have never been as sore as I was that Sunday. Normally, after a marathon or ultramarathon, my legs kill me. But after Lacrosse Quest 24, I had whole-body ache. All the game's stopping and starting had rubbed my feet raw. Then there were the knees. I had taken a couple of very dramatic tumbles and had used my knees to break my fall on the concrete. Not good. The calves and quads also got a going over, running up and down the arena floor for hours on end. Pass after pass and shot after shot gave my back, shoulders and arms a good work out.

We completed 24 hours of box lacrosse and achieved a brand new Guinness World Record. Of course, the original Indigenous lacrosse players would have played for longer, and in tougher circumstances! The final score was Donkeys (my team) 299 and Unicorns 296. I scored three goals, not bad for my first game.

Quest #3: By the Numbers

Lacrosse Quest 24 (April 27 – 28, 2012)
Objective: To play 24 hours of box lacrosse and set a Guinness World Record
Location: South Fish Creek Recreation Complex, Calgary, Alberta, Canada
Status: Guinness World Record set (24 hours, 2 minutes and 19 seconds)
Donations: $42,493
Matching funds: $127,479
Total raised: $169,972
Kids helped: 3,399
Funds application: Benin, West Africa

FOUR

Kraft Celebration Tour

"If life is a buffet, I'm still at the mac and cheese phase."
– JAROD KINTZ, author of *This Book Is Not for Sale*

Every year TSN and Kraft tour Canada to celebrate the culture in small towns and award a cash prize to the best town. In 2012 Kelly Kimmett – who would become instrumental to me in future quests – put together a proposal in order to enter the TSN–Kraft contest. A vote-off was held, and Cochrane beat Innisfail, another Alberta town that had bid for the award. The Celebration Tour came to town, I was featured in a video and the Town of Cochrane received $25,000.

In early June 2012 I received a call to go to the local Smitty's pancake house for a breakfast meeting. The call came from Alex Baum, whom I knew from the Cochrane Rotary Club. He wanted me to meet with Jack Tennant, the owner of the local newspaper the *Cochrane Eagle* and a huge supporter of Quests for Kids, and Dan Kroffat, whom I also knew.

Dan kicked off the meeting by telling a story. In early May the Canadian government announced that it would no longer be minting the penny. He had heard Finance Minister Jim Flaherty say that Canadians should donate their remaining pennies to charitable causes. This gave Dan, Alex and Jack an idea. They wanted to do a fundraiser called Ton of Pennies, in support of TriOil-Soccer Quest 42 and Right To Play. The Soccer Quest committee had been working diligently, and one member, Robin Mitchell, the manager of Spray Lake Sawmills Family Sports Centre, had talked to Russ Tripp, president of TriOil Resources, and had persuaded him to come on board as a Gold Sponsor. TriOil committed $10,000 to the event, with the proviso that the money was to be used to pay a Guinness adjudicator to oversee the attempt. The quest was coming up in October, and the more funds raised the better. I thought Ton of Pennies was a brilliant idea and went home to find out more about Canada's once-venerable penny.

According to the Royal Canadian Mint, the official term for the coin is the "one-cent piece," but, in practice, "penny" or "cent" are often used. Originally, a penny was a two-cent coin. But when that coin was discontinued, the word "penny" took over as the name for the new one-cent piece, probably because, up until 1858, Canada used British currency – the British pound, shilling and pence coinage – alongside U.S. decimal coins and Spanish milled dollars.

At that time in 2012, 30 billion pennies were in circulation – $300 million! I knew that 5,000 pennies ($50) would give a child a Right To Play program for one year. I figured out that 5,000 pennies weighed

27.6 pounds, and with 2,000 pounds to the ton, the Ton of Pennies fundraiser would help 72 children. On top of that, for every penny raised, Right To Play partners would add another three pennies, raising the number of kids encouraged to 288 for every ton collected.

Alex, Dan and Jack arranged a launch and press conference for Saturday, June 9, at Cochrane Toyota. There was a good crowd in attendance, and it was great to see so many kids from Cochrane Minor Soccer. They had a blast pouring handfuls of pennies into huge wine jars.

After the launch, soccer loomed large. The last two weeks of June were all about "the beautiful game." Sue and I watched every match played in the Euro 2012 Soccer Tournament and went out to support local soccer initiatives, including Cochrane Minor Soccer's Soccerfest on June 23, which dawned wet and chilly.

The games were played at Mitford and West Rock fields. In total, 53 teams turned up for the event, including ones from nearby Canmore and Redwood Meadows. The heavy mist didn't dampen the fun, and U-6 boys and girls got things off to a flying start.

The event was a fundraiser for Right To Play, and each team was asked to bring bags of pennies to donate to the Ton of Pennies initiative. Team after team poured their coins into large, clear containers, and we collected a total of 200 pounds. The winning team for pennies collected (98 pounds!) was the Lime Cobra U-13 girls' team.

On July 1 Sue and I headed to Redwood Meadows to take part in that community's Canada Day celebration and another Ton of Pennies fundraiser for Right To Play. Carol Scarratt, RTP supporter, had organized a float to collect the pennies for TriOil-Soccer Quest 42. The float had an 18-foot canoe on a trailer as well as a tipi covered with a huge Right To Play banner. Prior to the event, Carol and her friends had dropped off brown paper bags at every house in the community, asking people to donate their pennies. I joined a team of kids going from porch to porch, collecting the bags of coins. It was a terrific day. Carol and the penny gang collected 420 pounds.

As I drove home, I reflected on the Quests for Kids. It was halftime for this ten-quest initiative – time to catch my breath, take in some nutrients and go over what had happened in the first half and think about the strategy for the next half. In soccer the first half is at 45 minutes, in Quests for Kids my first half came at two and a half years. So how did the first half look?

1. Amount of time used: 2.5 years
2. Number of quests completed: 3
3. Amount raised: $518,572
4. Number of children helped: 10,371

As it turned out, this halftime coincided with me receiving an honour, one that encouraged me and showed that I was on the right track. On July 9, 2012, I was notified by my MP, Blake Richards, that on October 9 I would be receiving the Queen Elizabeth II Diamond Jubilee Medal. As Richards's letter says:

> This commemorative award was created to mark the 2012 celebrations of the 60th anniversary of Her Majesty the Queen of Canada's accession to the Throne. You are one of just 30 residents of the Wild Rose constituency selected to receive this prestigious honour, recognizing your contributions to community and country…What you all share is a commitment to service, a quality personified by Her Majesty, who has

served the Crown and all the Commonwealth countries with steadfast devotion over the past six decades.

I felt proud to be recognized, and the letter spurred me on in my efforts with the Quests for Kids.

In mid-July Sue and I visited our daughter Kristina and our grandkids, Autumn, then eight, and Nathan, three. We stayed at a lakeside resort where we canoed and swam. Every evening we fished while watching the sun go down. The bait of choice was hotdogs, and the catch was often crayfish, but it didn't matter. The pace was slow and the company enchanting.

We moved on from there to Toronto, where we attended the Right To Play fundraising Red Ball Gala at the Westin Harbour Castle. The guests of honour for the evening were four well-known sports personalities, golfers Ernie Els and Mike Weir, Olympic rower Silken Laumann, and NHL hockey legend Steve Yzerman.

When we entered the ballroom we could hardly fail to notice two tables populated with bottles from Ernie and Mike's wineries. Sue had a glass of the 2010 Mike Weir Sauvignon Blanc, and I tried the 2010 Ernie Els Big Easy Red. If I ever become a big shot, I think I'll open a brewery and serve my guests premium beers like Parnell Porter, Parnell Pilsner and Parnell Pale Ale.

A key part of the evening was to recognize the four special guests for their work helping children. In the spring of 2005, Canadian golf icon Mike Weir launched Mike Weir Estate Winery to showcase the world-class wines being made in Ontario's Niagara Peninsula and to support the Mike Weir Foundation, which Mike and his wife Bricia started in 2004. Proceeds from the sale of Weir wines go to assist children in physical, emotional and financial need.

In 2008 Ernie Els started to display the Autism Speaks logo on his golf bag after it was announced that his 5-year-old son Ben was autistic. In 2009 he launched an annual charity golf event, the Els for Autism Pro-Am. The first event, which featured many PGA Tour and Champion Tour golfers, raised $725,000 for the Learning Center, a non profit charter school for autistic children based in Jupiter, Florida. Ernie and his wife Liezl also established the Els Center of Excellence, which started to help build a new campus for the Learning Center but has since mushroomed into a $30-million plan to combine the school with a research facility.

When she retired from the sport in 1999, Silken Laumann had won three Olympic medals in rowing. She went on to be the spokesperson for GoodLife Kids and a board member of Right To Play International. She also wrote a book championing play: *Child's Play: Rediscovering the Joy of Play in Our Families and Communities.*

Steve Yzerman is involved with the Detroit Mercy Hospital and Make-a-Wish Foundation. He also supports kids on a personal level. A boy named Braxton met his hero, Steve, at the hospital before enduring eight major surgeries. Steve did not forget Braxton and, one evening, invited him and his dad to the playoffs in Detroit. One of Steve's friends, who worked for United Airlines, arranged for them to fly to Detroit, and the Red Wings put them up at a downtown hotel. Braxton was invited to sit in the penalty box during warm-ups, and Pavel Datsyuk shot pucks at him.

Each of the four guests received the Red Ball Award from Johann Koss, president and CEO of Right To Play International.

After finding out more about these individuals, and their accomplishments outside of their fields of sport, it reminded me of the Right

To Play motto: Look After Yourself, Look After One Another. This motto would also apply to an initiative happening closer to home, in Cochrane, where a group of people were gearing up to celebrate Alberta's "best town."

In 2008 Kraft got together with TSN and came up with an idea. They wanted to celebrate small-town Canada and support community projects. So they sent out a cross-country call for nominations for "best town." The winning community from each province and territory would receive $25,000 and host a community celebration.

In 2012 Cochrane vied with Innisfail for the Alberta prize. Kelly Kimmett, a local pharmacist, sent in an amazing application, in which he proposed that Cochrane would spend the $25,000 on the town's Mitford Park recreation area. Upgrades would include improvements to the soccer pitch, new bleachers for the fans, a

The Nuts and Bolts of PLAY

All PLAY programs include regular weekly activities for kids. The activities vary in each community but usually include leadership workshops, sport and recreation pursuits, chances to volunteer, community events, sport workshops and youth-led projects. It's all about creating positive change. Every community involved with PLAY also gets training and support in at least one of the following core programs: After School, Youth Leadership, Diabetes Prevention and Sport For Development (lacrosse is an example of a sport played in this program). Each community also has the chance to apply for additional workshops that help leaders enhance the core programs: baseball leagues, basketball clinics, female empowerment programs, hockey sessions, lacrosse leagues, soccer seminars and summer camps. All in all, PLAY inspires success!

refurbished band shell, a better ball-diamond concession and washrooms, improved lighting on the skating and fishing pond, portable rink dividers, and resurfacing of pathways for Cochrane's huge running festival, Footstock.

The centrepiece of Kimmett's suggested revamp was the construction of a storage/concession/media building on the shore of Mitford Pond, along with improved washrooms and a skate-changing area.

Each town entered would feature a local personality, and Kelly had mentioned me and my Marathon Quest 250 in the application. So I did a video shoot with TSN in Kananaskis Country, running around Barrier Lake, across a meadow and along a ridge in Peter Lougheed Park.

Kraft Dinner

Pasta and cheese casseroles have been included in cookbooks like the *Liber de Coquina* as early as the Middle Ages. Such casseroles were consumed only by the upper classes until around the 18th century, when they became fashionable in Paris.

At that time, future American President Thomas Jefferson encountered macaroni when on a trip to France and northern Italy. In 1793 Jefferson asked the American ambassador to Paris, William Short, to buy a machine for making it. Perhaps the machine didn't work well because Jefferson later imported both macaroni and Parmesan cheese for his own use. In 1802 he served a "macaroni pie" at a state dinner.

Kraft Dinner, known as Kraft Macaroni and Cheese in the United States and Macaroni Cheese in the UK, is a convenient form of this storied casserole. The original product was marketed in 1937 by the company now known as Kraft Foods.

In early July, the result was in. Cochrane, 154,000; Innisfail, 95,000. On August 12 Cochrane experienced a party like it had never seen before. It was great to see everyone come out and celebrate the community together. This celebration was like foreshadowing for Quest #5, TriOil-Soccer Quest, which would also bring the community together, this time around the beautiful game.

Over the years I've played many sports, but, at the age of 3, I was given one of the greatest gifts a child could receive: a soccer ball. I have vivid memories of building goal posts with my friends, Patrick and Vernon. They were made out of pieces of aluminum tubing we'd found at the local dump. We taped the pieces together then draped some old garden netting over the back. Many an evening was spent kicking the ball around.

My next memory of this game is going to watch my local soccer team, Plymouth Argyle. The city of Plymouth was only 32 kilometres from where I lived, but at the age of 11, taking the bus to Home Park, Argyle's ground, was a big adventure. Most of the times I went, it was raining and the highlight was having a hot cup of tea and a Cornish pasty at halftime. The biggest game I ever watched was when Santos, from Brazil, came to town. Over 37,000 watched as the world-famous Pele took to the pitch. It was an amazing game that, incredibly, Plymouth won, 3–2.

I kept playing through my teens, at Camborne School of Mines, Cornwall, and into my early 20s, in Kimberley, BC, and Pine Point, NT. Then I stopped. I took a 30-year break until August 2012, when I pulled out my old cleats and polished them up, anticipating the quest to come: breaking the Guinness World Record for the longest game of five-a-side soccer. Lucy Lovelock, from the Cochrane Rangers women's soccer team, had been working hard to recruit players. She sent me a tentative list. On Eh Team were Dee Dee Cook, Daran Fletcher, Sherry Grund, Terry Norman, me, Dena Sykes, Denean Thorsen and Cecily Woolrich. Team Red Quest consisted of Kira Alston, Ellen Anderson Penno, Andy Harris, Rochelle Nydokus, Maria Perkovic, David Savage, Caitlin Smid and Matt Waicek. With a month to go before the GWR event, the key was for all the players to stay healthy. Unfortunately, for one of them, this would not be the case.

During the latter part of August and into September, I headed out and played. One evening I bounced the ball around with members of the Cochrane Rangers men's recreational league. We finished the evening with a pickup game against the women's team. Just like when I was a kid, it was getting dark by the time we wrapped up. Some things never change.

Before I could think more about Soccer Quest, though, I had some training to do in preparation for Quest #4, the run around Rarotonga. On Labour Day Sue and I headed over to Nose Hill Park in northwest Calgary where Jason Webb from Downunder Travel had organized a Back to School Fun Run in aid of RTP. There were 5- and 10-kilometre races; the big attraction for all those who had registered was to have their name entered into a draw to win a trip for two to the Cook Islands.

That morning I only had time to run the 5-K race as I had to get back to Cochrane by 10:30 a.m. to participate in the Labour Day Parade. The fun run at Nose Hill was definitely an undulating course. Some even called it "rolling." I thought it was a blast and finished in 27 minutes and 51 seconds. Not bad for an old fella.

By now the Ton of Pennies initiative had netted 1,500 pounds of pennies; only 500 pounds to go. The week before the Labour Day Parade, the *Cochrane Eagle* had included paper "penny" bags in the newspaper and asked residents to fill them up and bring them out to the parade. I rode in Cochrane Toyota's chuckwagon float with ten kids. Along the route, we collected the bags of pennies. By the end of the parade, the floor of the truck was full of coins. The Ton of Pennies initiative eventually raised $6,100 for Right To Play. Now that's a lot of pennies.

PLAY Community Mentor Training

In every PLAY program community, Right To Play hires a local youth worker to lead the program, who becomes the PLAY Community Mentor. At the start of each program year (September–June), Right To Play brings all of the Community Mentors together for a week of training workshops. These workshops don't just teach the power of play; they give the Community Mentors the opportunity to experience the power for themselves. Mentor training helps leaders use play as a tool to teach essential life skills, such as teamwork, focus, communication and healthy living.

In 2015 PLAY welcomed Community Mentors from across Canada to the training workshops: British Columbia, Alberta, Manitoba and Ontario. The workshops not only give the leaders ideas for programming but they also provide them with a network of other leaders in other Aboriginal communities. Elders join the new and returning mentors, giving insight to discussions and providing an atmosphere of emotional and spiritual safety. Community Mentors go back to their communities feeling engaged, valued and connected. As one participant said, "I know I made some awesome new connections. I stepped WAY out of my comfort zone a few times and it made me braver, more confident."

FIVE

Mad Dogs and Englishmen

"When a great adventure is offered, you don't refuse it."
– AMELIA EARHART, aviatrix, quoted by
Valerie Moolman in *Women Aloft*

Quest #4 had me heading off to Rarotonga in the Cook Islands. My challenge was to run three times around this desert island, a total of 100 kilometres. This couldn't be all that bad, right?

On September 16 I headed off to "paradise" to embark on Quest #4. The first leg of the journey would take me to Los Angeles and then, after a ten-hour stopover, it was on to Rarotonga. I travelled with Jason Webb and Monica Zurowski, the managing editor of the *Calgary Herald*, who was doing an article on the Cook Islands and my participation in the Rarotonga Road Race.

I must admit, I was looking forward to this quest. The first three had beaten me up. Hours, days, months of running, netball and lacrosse had drained me both mentally and physically. Now I was about to run around a tropical island for 16 hours. No hills, no −30°C, just the swaying of palm trees and the gentle lapping of waves on the shore. What could go wrong? I was about to find out.

Upon arrival, we were driven to the Edgewater Resort, aptly named as my room faced the ocean. After a leisurely breakfast, Jason and I went over the details of my itinerary. First up was an interview with the Cook Island news station, during which I told reporter Calida all about Marathon Quest 250. Calida was writing an article about my race around the island.

Later in the day, I decided to check out my surroundings and get a feel for what challenges I might encounter on the run. It didn't take me long to realize that one of them would be the traffic. Cars and scooters zip along the narrow roads, and you really need your wits about you in order to avoid them. I hoped my headlight would be bright enough for the portions of the route I would have to run at night.

Another obstacle I'd have to contend with was the number of animals on the roads. Pigs, cows, dogs and goats, not to mention the chickens scurrying about. On the island they say there are more chickens than people, and I can well believe it.

An odd concern that surfaced during my recce was coconuts. The sides of the road were strewn with them. They had fallen from great heights and exploded. Apparently, more Australians are killed by falling coconuts than shark attacks.

After 30 minutes of wandering, I headed back to the resort in time to shower and "dress" for supper. I use the term loosely, as it simply meant putting on a clean shirt and shorts. I met the rest of the group in the bar and then it was off to a "plantation dinner." The meal was cooked in the home of an island resident named Louis, and he showed us around his garden. He grows a huge variety of produce, all of which he uses in the dishes he cooks.

The next day, after another television interview, Jason and I sat down to meet with Krissy, one of the race organizers. We discussed the logistics of running 100 kilometres and my requirements for the run. Joining us were Eni and her daughter Siniva, who was the administrator for the Cook Islands Olympic Committee and had just returned from London with the national team. Eni and Siniva explained that their ancestors were originally from England, and that their surname, Marsters, has a link to Queen Victoria. The island clearly has a long history of settlement and colonization.

In fact, Lonely Planet's *Rarotonga* tells us that Rarotongans' trace their history back around 1,400 years. Included in that history is the story of To'i, the 11th-century king who built the island's ancient road, Ara Metua. At this point, the island seems to have been populated mostly by settlers from current-day French Polynesia. In 1773, after explorer James Cook sighted the group of islands, he spent four years charting them and, in true English tradition, attached a series of "dull, irrelevant names to wonderful places." It wasn't until 50 years later that a Russian cartographer, Johann von Krusenstern, published an atlas in which he renamed the islands in honour of James Cook. Later that day, Jason suggested I have my own transport for getting around and he rented me a scooter. So, after obtaining a licence from the local police station, I was set to go. I followed Jason to a great little beach café where I enjoyed a big chunk of Mahi Mahi in a sandwich. As Jason had some errands to run, I decided to take a spin around the island on my own. The speed limit is 50 kilometres/hour, so I tootled along, checking out the race course as I passed the painted kilometre markers. I spotted a couple of areas where falling coconuts might be a serious issue. It only took me 45 minutes to circumnavigate the island and then it was back to the resort for a meeting with three highly accomplished runners from Japan.

Mr. Takahashi was the leader of the group. He organizes trips to marathons around the world and specializes in lesser-known events. Another member, Mr. Kokubu, was 67 years old and had completed 500 marathons, while the third, Mr. Niida, was 76 and had won the 70-plus age category at marathon races in Jamaica and Israel.

I met them at the airport, along with Kelly Pick, a top-level triathlete who lives on the island. Jason had told us that the Japanese runners had wanted to loosen up after their 20-hour flight and were keen to run with Kelly and me.

On arrival, they changed into their running gear and, as planned, we ran the 3.5 kilometres from the airport to the resort. Most striking was Mr. Niida, who donned a running kimono. The run went well, and we later got together for supper.

Before making our way to eat at the Kiku Hut, we stopped in at the Roadhouse, as the Japanese guys wanted to meet some locals. We ordered a beer, and few moments later a young woman came over to our table and said, "Konnichiwa." It turned out she had begun learning Japanese when she was 15 and had spent the past three years studying in Japan. I think the guys were relieved to meet her, as only Mr. Takahashi could speak English.

The next day, I met Meghan Mutrie from Sky Sports New Zealand, who wanted to spend the day with me and do a series of interviews. We joined Eni at a local stadium to watch students from the Prince of Wales Primary School compete in their sports day. While there, Meghan introduced me to Kevin Iro, who had played rugby league for the Cook Islands and New Zealand and also as a professional in Leeds and Wigan in the UK. A top-class player. He was now retired and putting his skills to use coaching a group of young adults – he was essentially Rarotonga's version of a PLAY Community Mentor, just a bit older.

That afternoon, Kevin kindly invited Meghan and me to attend a pig roast. We enjoyed a feast of fish, pork and a variety of vegetables. Unfortunately, I couldn't stay too long as I had a Rotary meeting to attend that evening. At the meeting, I was greeted by the club's president. I spoke about Marathon Quest 250 and received a great response.

My first introduction to Rotary was in 1989 when I was still living in Sudbury, Ontario, and working for Falconbridge Limited. My boss asked if I wanted to apply to join a Rotary Cultural Exchange trip to Australia. I said yes, applied, was interviewed and selected. Along with four other non-Rotarians, I spent six weeks visiting Rotary clubs along the east coast of Australia. We spoke about our individual areas of expertise.

The next time I spoke at a Rotary club was 20 years later, in 2009. I was living in Cochrane by then and went to our local club, requesting help with Marathon Quest 250. Rotary's motto is "Service Above Self," and it certainly came through for me in 2010 when the club agreed to print 60 maps of my virtual route across Canada and distribute them to schools in Cochrane and Calgary. Two years later, I joined the club and Rotary has supported my quests ever since.

The day after my Rotary speech, I did some more filming with Meghan. She had it in her head that I was some sort of running guru, "The Marathon Whisperer," and wanted me to share three secrets of running. Her idea for the shoot was for us to trek into the rainforest, and I would play the role of a running holy man whom she'd interview in a cave or perched on a giant rock. I loved it. We made our way toward the entrance of the Cross-Island Trek but not before meeting a woodcutter, Michael Tovriolle, whose niece had made a dress for the Duchess of Cambridge.

Meghan and I parked at the trail head and started to walk. It began to rain, but we trudged on. However, as the rain got heavier and heavier, we realized we weren't going to be able to shoot much film, so we turned around. We had just got back onto open trail when the sun appeared, so we decided to climb a short distance back to a huge rock we'd spotted on the way in and do a quick shoot from there. The rain returned, but we managed to shield the camera with a giant palm leaf. Meghan asked me to reveal my three secrets to being a successful runner and I told her: comfortable shoes, good nutrition and hydration. My take-away line was "Run long and prosper."

We returned to Avarua and enjoyed a well-earned coffee.

Next, I went to the race-package pickup and prepared to run the 5-kilometre race, which was part of the overall event. The theme for this fun run was Dress Up. Interesting costumes emerged: the pussy-cat women, two fairies and a Japanese man who had a model toilet on his head. Unfortunately, I had come unprepared and didn't have a costume. At 5 p.m. the gun went off and away we went. A lead group

Sheshegwaning PLAY Participants Change Their Community One Step at a Time

Since 2012 Community Mentor Leonard Genereux has been leading youth in Sheshegwaning First Nation's PLAY program, seeing participants "take control of their own lives." Leonard noted that these same youth were leading real change in their community.

Sixteen-year-old Kaitlynn Tomaselli, for example, is a gymnast who long yearned to take part in her school's gymnastics club, but the school is over an hour's drive from her home and she would have no way to get home after practices. She noticed that other youth in her community had the same problem, and so she took the reins and started a shuttle service. She recruited her father and uncle to take turns driving youth home from their after-school activities in a community-owned van.

Kaitlynn says, "More people are starting to be more involved in school whether it has to do with school help, clubs or sports." By participating in the school's activities, youth are able "to build new relationships with other students who may share the same interests."

Another Sheshegwaning PLAY participant, Dietrah Hoppe, expressed a common desire for an ice rink in the community. With Leonard's support and encouragement, Dietrah took her idea for a rink to some community organizations, and her plan was approved. Other youth jumped in to help, as well as parents and others. In fact, families that usually didn't get along were soon working together to make the rink a reality. Now, the entire community has a place to skate, play hockey and even run PLAY Hockey for Development programs.

"Youth in the community are taking initiative on issues that are important to them," Leonard says. "When they realize they are successful and the response that it generates from the community, it builds their self-esteem and confidence that they can really make a difference."

dashed off, with the rest of us bringing up the rear. At the 1-kilometre point, a shout went up, the lead group had gone the wrong way. So the group I was with took over the lead. The race turned out to be shorter than 5 kilometres, but I wasn't complaining. A group of us made our way to Trader Jack's and watched an outrigger come in before heading home.

The island has a public bus system. On the front of a bus it says either "clockwise" or "anti-clockwise." To be honest, it really doesn't matter, as there is no wrong way on a circular route. It was time to catch the clockwise bus and return to the resort and bed.

At 5 a.m. I was up, unable to sleep and relieved that the big day had arrived. After eating breakfast, I got ready for my trip to Tereora College. The three Japanese gentlemen were joining Jason, Meghan and I for a presentation, but, whereas we drove the 3 kilometres, they jumped on their bikes. On arrival, we met Mr. Bali, the principal. He explained that the college held Grades 9 to 13 and from there students could pursue post-secondary education in New Zealand. In total, there were 650 students. We went into the main hall, and I was surprised to see that boys and girls had to use separate entrances and that the boys sat on the right-hand side of the hall and the girls on the left. After a prayer, led by the pastor, Mr. Bali introduced me and I gave a 15-minute, condensed version of my story, so far. We were then treated to a catwalk fashion show, presented by the "Create Your Own" class. The ensembles were amazing and a real highlight for the students.

I managed to get a few hours' sleep before eating my pre-race meal of chicken wraps and Diet Coke. Resting in my room, I switched on the TV. My luck was in. They were showing a soccer match, between

AC Milan and Manchester United. AC Milan won 3–2, coming twice from behind. Before I knew it, it was 8:15 p.m. and time to head out and begin my 100-kilometre run.

As Jason, Meghan and I proceeded to the 24-kilometre mark, which was my starting point, the rain pounded on the windshield. Not a good start. As we approached our destination, we spotted a vehicle up ahead. It was Eni and a friend. They would follow me on my first two laps.

Soon I was standing next to the large "24" painted on the road. I had made all my preparations the night before. My hydration pack held 2 litres of water and Carbo-Pro, and I had another 2 litres in my water bottles. I also had electrolytes, three bananas, toilet paper, Band-Aids, my camera and the key to my hotel room.

A small group of people stood on the side of the road and counted down, "5, 4, 3, 2, 1" – I was off. It was still raining, but I was confident it would ease off, as it had the previous couple of days. This was the start to Quest #4, and as I headed into the dark, with my headlight throwing a dim spot on the road, I knew it was going to be a long night. Each loop of the island measures 31 kilometres. In order to complete the 100 kilometres, I had to run three and a bit – 7 kilometres – times around the island. Members of the organizing committee had painted big white numbers on the pavement to mark the kilometres. There was no chance of missing one.

I soon passed markers 25 and 26. The rain was continuous, and my socks and shoes became soaked. I knew this was going to cause big problems later on. I reached marker 0 after 45 minutes, and I was feeling wet but good. Only three loops to go.

In addition to the clockwise/anti-clockwise bus, there is another bus service that I had been told about: the party or pub-crawl bus that helps stop drinking and driving. The first one passed me at 11 p.m. The strobe lights were flashing and techno pop was pounding.

I was told to be aware of dogs as I ran. However, I have to say that the island has the friendliest dogs I have ever met. They seem to practise "Adopt-a-Visitor." They weren't aggressive or pushy, just friendly. I made a friend on my first loop at kilometre 15. He trotted next to me for 20 minutes then turned around. I would meet him again on my next two loops.

I completed my first loop in 3 hours and 50 minutes and was feeling good. When I returned to the start point at 4 hours and 45 minutes, Val was waiting to join me. She had signed up for Cook Island Quest 100 and had been fundraising for Right To Play. This would be Val's longest run, twice around the island, but she had been training hard.

At around the 40-kilometre mark, I began to have problems; my feet were still soaked and, as the rain hadn't ceased, they hadn't had a chance to dry off. The puddles were becoming bigger and bigger, and there was no avoiding them.

I started to slow down and could feel big blisters beginning to form across the balls of my feet. I'd had this issue in two previous ultra races, the Sinister Seven and Iron Legs, and it's very painful – but there was nothing I could do about it. Our objective was to get around the island and back to the start line by 5:30 a.m., when the official race began, but I knew time was slipping away. I told Val to go on, but she stuck with me.

We arrived at 6:45 a.m., and the other runners had already set off. Val went ahead, and I started to walk. My feet were in a bad way, and I was starting to fall asleep standing up. Then an angel arrived riding a bicycle. Her name was Toru – I had met her at the Rotary Club meeting the previous Wednesday. She saw the condition I was in and asked if I would like a coffee and chocolate bar. At that moment I would have run 100 kilometres for a coffee and chocolate bar. Soon the sugar and caffeine kicked in, and I started to feel better. She also kept a conversation going. I think she could see I was dead tired.

Toru was born on the island and attended university in Fiji. She was currently working at a printer's and was a sports nut. She played soccer, rugby and golf, and took part in triathlons. She asked me to guess her age. I thought she was in her mid-20s. It turned out she was 39.

As we continued walking around the final loop, she picked bananas off the trees and fed me. She gave me a coconut with a hole in it, and I drank the milk. The rain continued, and I was losing body heat, big time. I was starting to shiver. I asked Toru if she had a jacket I could use, and, another miracle, she pulled a waterproof jacket out of her backpack. It was a little short in the arms but fitted around the body. It turned out to be a life saver as, by this time, I was really beginning to suffer from the cold.

At 1:15 p.m. I saw the 30-kilometre marker on the road for the third time. Ninety-nine kilometres done, only one to go. After 16 hours, 21 minutes and 37 seconds, I shuffled across the finish line, where a small group of supporters were waiting to cheer me in. I was given a flower garland, an engraved shell medal and another drink of coconut milk. Then Victor, from Cook Island Tourism, drove me back to the resort.

After a hot bath, I lay down on my bed, reminiscing about the run and soon fell fast asleep. I woke to attend the final event, a Polynesian Evening, held at the resort. We were only able to stay for a couple of hours before heading off to the airport for our long journey home. Jason had kindly booked me into business class, and within five minutes of take-off, I was sleeping like a baby.

I woke up with a jolt and for a moment wondered where I was. The cabin was dark, and the only noise was the hum of the engines. I tried to get back to sleep but couldn't. My mind was racing and not in a good way. The fourth quest was done. I thought it would be a walk in the park – in this case a run around the island – however my feet were telling me it was far more than that. They had been soaked for 16 hours and chunks of white and shrivelled skin had started to peel off. Normally, this wouldn't have been a big problem. I would tend to them, and over several weeks they would return to normal. The trouble was I didn't have weeks, in fact I only had 13 days to get my feet in shape for Quest #5.

Quest #4: By the Numbers

Cook Island Quest 100 (September 21 –22, 2012)
Objective: To run around Rarotonga three times and a bit, 100 kilometres.
Location: Rarotonga, Cook Islands
Status: Completed 100 kilometres (16 hours, 21 minutes and 37 seconds)
Donations: $7,888
Matching funds: $23,664
Total: $31,552
Kids helped: 631
Funds application: Benin, West Africa

SIX

Game of Two Halves

"Some people think football [soccer] is a matter of
life and death. I assure you it's much more
important than that."
– BILL SHANKLEY, manager of Liverpool Football Club
(1959–1974), speaking to a hotel clerk in Brussels

*My first love was soccer, and when the Cochrane Rangers agreed
to help me attempt a Guinness World Record for the longest game
of indoor soccer, I was over the moon. This was Quest #5, and one
I was really looking forward to.*

A great team worked together to make Soccer Quest a reality. Three
key members were Robin Mitchell at Spray Lake Sawmills Family
Sport Centre, Lucy Lovelock from the Cochrane Rangers team
and Alison Temple from Cochrane Minor Soccer. I also had Nick

Edwards, who had emailed me early on to say he would "love to play in [the] world-record breaker." The problem was, at 12 years old, Nick was officially too young to participate. I went to see him at his home and offered him a position on the organizing committee. I explained that his role would be to see how we could include members of Cochrane Minor Soccer and make them feel part of the event. He accepted.

After I had recruited all the committee members I thought I'd need, we held our first meeting. A plan began to materialize. The Cochrane Rangers would be the lead organization, supported by the folks from Minor Soccer. Robin offered to make enquiries with the aim of securing sponsorship for the event. This was going to be a huge undertaking, and so we agreed to set the event's date in October 2012.

Robin did find a sponsor, as you already know, in the form of Tri-Oil, which allowed us to bring in an adjudicator from Guinness. By the time I arrived back from the Cook Islands, everything was ready. Although my feet were in a bad way from my run around Rarotonga, I was still excited to launch myself into Soccer Quest.

At 4 p.m. on October 5, we all gathered at the centre. Everyone was pumped and ready to get going. However, there was disappointment for one player. On October 2 Terry Norman had emailed me to say that a knee injury would prevent him from playing, saying: "Believe me when I tell you how disappointed I am. I would suffer through if [the injury] occurred during the event, but to start out on Friday knowing that it will fail at some point or that the pain and/ or swelling will overcome its playability (this already happens if I try jogging to the end of the block) leaves me with no choice but to be pissed off and concerned about you guys and the cause. Maybe I just need an injection of Martin." Fortunately, Terry had found a replacement, Jason Smith, and at precisely 6 p.m. on Friday, October 5, 2012, the whistle blew and the game was on.

Everyone started off by running around like chickens with their heads cut off. I knew we wouldn't last four hours like this, never mind 42. I suggested we slow down. Some listened to my advice, some didn't, and I knew there would be a price to pay later on. The other reason I wanted to start off slowly was the condition of my feet. They were still pretty tender. The hours ticked by, and goal after goal was scored. Lucy had scheduled each player on an eight-hours on, four-hours off rotation. We tried to nap in the dressing rooms. But, to be honest, none of us got much sleep.

At 3 p.m. the next day, a huge cheer went up when we reached halftime: 21 hours done; 21 hours to go. Fatigue began to set in. The play was down to a crawl, but the goals kept coming. The toughest time was in the early hours of the second day. Sleep deprivation was affecting everyone.

At 12:01 p.m. on Sunday, October 7, 2012, MP Blake Richards blew the whistle, bringing to an end 42 hours and 1 minute of five-a-side soccer. I was on the substitute's bench as the shrill note went up, and everyone at the centre burst into cheers. The celebrations began with the players hugging and giving high-fives, as Robin Mitchell called together the two teams and introduced Michael Empric, Guinness World Record adjudicator. Michael congratulated all involved and announced that a new record had, officially, been set.

Injuries and fatigue had taken their toll, but no one had quit. The final score was Eh Team, 381; Team Red Quest, 346. But we were all winners. A Guinness World Record had come to Cochrane, and over 2,600 children had been given the gift of a Right To Play program for one year.

Neskantaga After School Program

Aaron Yellowhead understands the value of education and hard work. A former Community Mentor in Neskantaga First Nation, Aaron passed on these values every day to the children who participated in his PLAY After School Program.

Aaron joined the PLAY team in 2013, but he had already been empowering youth in Neskantaga for many years. At the Better Futures program, Aaron helped young people in his community of 300 on-reserve residents learn to lead healthier lives. With PLAY, he strived to increase youth engagement in school.

In 2013 Aaron aimed to incorporate homework time and educational activities into his program. He and school teachers jointly agreed to Aaron running an additional night of programming on Thursdays, on top of his usual Monday, Friday and Saturday programming. Thursday's PLAY program encouraged kids to stay for the homework club that happened just before PLAY kicked in that evening.

There were 30 students between the ages of 6 and 13 attending PLAY programs in the community. They received the time and support they needed to complete their homework. Aaron ran games that improved focus and concentration, as well as learning games, for those who did not have homework assignments. The program's success was measured by the kids' constant question – every day they asked Aaron, "When is Right To Play?"

That evening, a group of us took Michael Empric out for supper. He told us that this record had been one of the best run and documented of any he had adjudicated. He continued that the success rate for approved records is only 5 per cent and most fail on the documentation side. Julie Arnold, Lucy Lovelock and Sarah Tas had made sure everything ran like clockwork and that all the event's supporting documents were correct. Volunteers turned up at the appointed times, the appropriate paperwork was satisfactorily completed and the required video evidence was recorded. Team members were provided with hot and tasty breakfasts, dinners and suppers – the knockout punch was the special delivery of Banana Buzz smoothies, brought in at the 11th hour from Jugo Juice.

That night, as I made my way home, I reflected on the three quests that had been completed in 2012. It would not have been possible without the help of hundreds of people volunteering for and donating money to a wonderful cause.

Over the following week, I received a number of emails from the Soccer Quest players, saying how much they had enjoyed the experience and what it had meant to them. One, in particular, goalkeeper Dena Sykes, struck home:

> First and foremost, a HUGE thank you for the amount of
> work you put in to our Soccer Quest 42 weekend!
> I realize I am part of a very historical and exciting event
> and I surpassed my fundraising goal, which is the icing on
> the cake! We were taken care of in such a great way and at
> no point did I ever believe this opportunity would fail – the
> well-executed meetings, the guidance from Martin regarding

fundraising, the support, Jo mothering and encouraging us and the actual event – everything went amazingly well. I had an excellent partner in Dee Dee and our laughter kept us both very motivated.

After a very long sleep I was googling Guinness and found out some interesting facts.

I am the only Thalidomide victim (soon to be on record) to hold a Guinness World Record. That, in itself, is exciting for me, but here's the very interesting part; in July 1957, Distillers Company signed a 16-year contract with Grunenthal (the makers of Thalidomide) to market the drug and ordered 6,000 tablets for clinical trial. (The rest, of course, is history. Thalidomide was not the wonder drug it was promoted to be, and after 10 months it became very apparent how toxic it was). In August 1954, the first compilation of the Guinness Book of Records was printed and in 1986, GUINNESS purchased Distillers Company and, unfortunately, the link with Thalidomide. Currently, Guinness is "doing the right thing" by supporting "Thalidomide victims" (I prefer "Thalidomider" as opposed to "Thalidomide victim," but I am quoting an article) in the UK, even though they were not in any way responsible for manufacturing the drug.

In two weeks, I will be joining approximately 84 surviving Thalidomiders in Ottawa to celebrate our 50 years together, and I will share these fascinating facts. Although I am one of a few visually less affected Thalidomiders, I am honoured that I was given an opportunity to break a record AND support an amazing charity AND find a positive link in a piece of my history…cool, eh?

The next quest – a hockey game – would not take place until early 2013. In the meantime, I had a trip to Toronto and another marathon to prepare for.

In mid-October 2012 I flew to Toronto. I had three objectives: give a copy of my first book, *Marathon Quest*, to Right To Play CEO Johann Koss; compete in Bonsai the Don, a trail race with a twist; and run the Scotiabank Waterfront Marathon. I flew out on a Thursday morning, fatigued and still feeling the effects from the 42-hour soccer game

My meeting with Johann was scheduled for 11:30 a.m. the next day. I had meet him a number of times before, and he had run with me in Toronto on marathon #154 of Marathon Quest 250. Sarah Stern, my RTP contact, took me up to his office. She knocked on his door, and he came out joined by Clara Hughes. Clara has been one of my inspirations for working with Right To Play. In 2006, after winning the gold medal in speed skating at the Turin Winter Olympics, she donated $10,000 to the organization, providing play-based programs for many children. I happened to have two copies of *Marathon Quest* with me, and I was happy to be able to give her a copy.

That afternoon I headed down to the marathon expo and picked up my race package. I chatted with John Stanton, founder of Running Room, who wrote a review for *Marathon Quest*. Then I spied one of my all-time heroes, Fauja Singh, over at the speakers' stage. In 2011, at the age of 100, Fauja ran a marathon, the first centurion ever to do so. This year he planned to run a 5-kilometre "victory lap" at the Toronto Marathon.

The day before the marathon, I headed to the Don Valley Parkway for a very special event. A group called Preparing the Trail had organized a three-hour trail run that my buddy David Houghton and I decided to do together. The twist in the run was that, at some point during the race, participants had to plant two trees. Preparing the Trail is a grassroots, environmentally active, not-for-profit organization that uses the power of sport to educate and empower people. It also supports its charitable partners, Right To Play and Trees Ontario. This organization was right up my alley.

The 5.5-kilometre loop followed the Don Valley's Crother's Woods Trail. The scenery was spectacular, and the kilometres flew by. David put the hammer down, completed 30 kilometres, planted two trees

Athlete Ambassador for Right To Play: Clara Hughes

Clara Hughes is a Canadian cyclist and speed skater, who has won multiple Olympic medals in both sports. As a result of her sports successes and her humanitarian efforts, she was named to both the Order of Manitoba and as an Officer of the Order of Canada. Clara is a dedicated advocate and Athlete Ambassador for Right To Play and has served on the organization's international board of directors. She is also the national spokesperson for the Bell Let's Talk Mental Health initiative, and she uses her past struggles with depression to relate to others and to help combat the stigma associated with mental health issues. Since 2013 Clara has scheduled annual bike rides across Canada to raise awareness about mental health. She published her memoir, Open Heart, Open Mind, in 2015.

and finished first. His prize? A Bonsai tree. I completed 19 kilometres, just the right amount for me in preparation for the next day's marathon.

Sunday morning came around quickly enough. As the gun went off, 14,000 of us headed out onto the streets of Toronto. I planned to run a five-hour marathon, but I was feeling good and, although the effects of the previous day's trail run had started to hit me, as I crossed into the 30-plus-kilometre zone, I hung in and finished in 4 hours, 40 minutes and 28 seconds.

Arriving back in Cochrane, there wasn't much time to rest. In fact, with the New York Marathon scheduled for November 4, all I could really do was start my taper and make sure that I didn't get injured. Little did I know there were storm clouds on the horizon.

Quest #5: By the Numbers

TriOil-Soccer Quest 42 (October 5–7, 2012)

Objective: To play 42 hours of five-a-side soccer and set a Guinness World Record

Location: Spray Lake Sawmills Family Sports Centre, Cochrane, Alberta, Canada

Status: Guinness World Record set (42 hours and 1 minute)

Donations: $35,704

Matching funds: $107,112

Total: $142,816

Kids helped: 2,856

Funds application: Benin, West Africa

SEVEN

Hurricane Sandy

"Leave your comfort zone. Go stretch
yourself for a good cause."
– KOBI YAMADA, author of
What Do You Do with an Idea?

*Sue and I planned to have a relaxing few days in New York, one
day of which would have me running the city's famous marathon.
But things didn't turn out quite as we'd expected.*

By late October 2012, I was in the midst of preparing for the New
York Marathon, a race that had been on my radar for a number of
years. I figured this run would be right up there with the Boston
Marathon (which I ran in 2004, 2008 and 2010). I had previously
discovered that entry into the New York run could be gained in one
of two ways: by lottery or time qualification. I could secure a place

by running a sub 1-hour 40-minute half-marathon. In 2003 I ran the Toronto Water Front Half Marathon in 1 hour, 30 minutes and 1 second, so I decided to enter the Last Chance Half. The race took place on November 13, 2011, and fortunately the pathways were snow-free. The route took us along the Bow River in Calgary, and I came in with a time of 1 hour, 37 minutes and 14 seconds. I was thrilled.

Then Hurricane Sandy hit America's east coast. Mid-morning on November 1, our flight to New York left Calgary. Having spent the previous four days following events there, we knew about the devastation the storm had caused. I contacted Westin's head office and was told that, fortunately for us, our hotel was one of the few that still had power and was open. I felt a bit unsure about whether or not to go ahead, but then I received an email from the race organizers, the New York Road Runners, saying that Mayor Bloomberg had announced that the ING New York City Marathon would proceed as planned and be dedicated to "the City of New York, the victims of the hurricane, and their families."

The email went on to report that plans would be adjusted for the race day, as a result of the storm's impact. The focus would be on the Sunday marathon, and Friday night's opening ceremony and Saturday's Dash to the Finish Line 5K were cancelled. The organizing committee had established ways for runners to give through charitable donations.

Upon reading the email, Sue and I decided to go.

When we arrived, parts of the city were still in total darkness, and there were no lights in the tunnels. Our taxi driver told us that many parts of the city were still without power. By the time we got to our hotel, it was midnight in Cochrane and we were exhausted.

New York Marathon

Fred Lebow founded the New York Marathon in 1970, with a course consisting of running loops around Central Park. Today the course covers all five boroughs of the city, beginning on Staten Island, in Fort Wadsworth, near the approach to the Verrazano-Narrows Bridge, which is closed to traffic for the event. Runners use both sides of the upper level of the bridge and the westbound side of the lower level. At the beginning of the race, the bridge is filled with runners, creating a dramatic spectacle.

After descending the bridge, the course winds through Brooklyn, along Fourth Avenue and Bedford Avenue, for about 18 kilometres. Runners pass through Bay Ridge, Sunset Park, Park Slope, Bedford-Stuyvesant, Williamsburg and Greenpoint.

At 21.1 kilometres, runners cross the Pulaski Bridge, marking both the halfway point and the entrance into Long Island City, Queens. After about 4 kilometres in Queens, runners cross the East River via Queensboro Bridge into Manhattan. Here many runners begin to tire, as the climb up the bridge is perhaps the difficult point in the marathon.

After about 26 kilometres, runners reach Manhattan. In this section, participants head north on First Avenue then cross briefly into the Bronx on Willis Avenue Bridge before returning to Manhattan on Madison Avenue Bridge. Runners proceed south through Harlem, down Fifth Avenue into Central Park. At the southern end of the park, the route crosses Central Park South, where thousands of people cheer runners on during the last stretch. At Columbus Circle, the race re-enters the park and finishes outside Tavern on the Green.

In 2008 Canadian Actor Ryan Reynolds ran the marathon in a very respectable 3 hours, 50 minutes and 22 seconds in order to raise money for Parkinson's in honour of his father, who suffered from the disease. In a *Huffington Post* article, he pledged to "join thousands of other men and women to march in lockstep solidarity toward searing psychic pain and physical humiliation."

Sue and I didn't know what to do. On the news and in the papers there was so much negativity about the marathon going ahead. After breakfast, we headed out and walked around Manhattan Midtown. Two blocks south of our hotel the lights were out and the streets deserted.

At midday, we went to the Right To Play office and met one of their representatives, Ally. I had wanted to meet her to talk about RTP's recent activities. However, our conversation quickly turned to the destruction caused by Hurricane Sandy. Ally explained that the area where she lived was without power and she had spent two days and nights on her own, with nothing but candles and a wind-up radio, listening to the BBC World Service. She had returned to work on the Thursday, but found it really scary going home, as 70 per cent of people in her area had left. There was no street lighting, and the elevator in her apartment building wasn't working. She decided to spend that night sleeping on the office floor and was then going to book into a hotel, but not for long because she was flying to Rwanda the following Sunday with RTP. On our way out of the building, we chatted with Pascal, who was on duty at the security desk. He told us that he lived an hour and a half out of the city, had no power at home and had only just made it into work, as the transport system was barely coping.

At the race expo, I picked up my race package, but by now we were concerned. By noon on Friday, Mayor Michael Bloomberg was insisting that the race would be good for the city, it would lift people's spirits and show that the city could rise above the tragedy. I picked up a copy of the *New York Post*, whose headline screamed "Abuse of Power." Apparently, the New York Road Runners had rented two large generators for the media tent at the marathon, and it was felt that they should be used for sending power to homes instead. The newspaper's article also criticized the use of race volunteers, who would be cleaning up after the race, when they could, instead, be helping in other areas of the city.

Indeed, people in Staten Island and the Rockaways had no power, no heat, no hot food. Many houses had been completely destroyed by the storm or fires, and some people were having to gut their houses because all their belongings had been ruined by water. We were hearing some truly heartbreaking stories and understood why some people were angry.

On Saturday, the *Post*'s headline read "Light Comes On, Bloomberg Cancels Marathon," and we received another email from the New York Road Runners, confirming that the race would not go ahead:

> The decision was made after it became increasingly apparent that the people of our city and the surrounding tristate area were still struggling to recover from the damage wrought by the recent extreme weather conditions. That struggle, fueled by the resulting extensive and growing media coverage antagonistic to the marathon and its participants, created conditions that raised concern for the safety of both those working to produce the event and its participants. While holding the race would not have required diverting resources from the recovery effort, it became clear that the apparent widespread perception to the contrary had become the source of controversy and division. Neither New York

Road Runners nor the City could allow a controversy over the marathon to result in a dangerous situation or to distract attention from all the critically important work that is being done to help New York City recover from the storm.

The organizers went on to write that they were "redeploying" the marathon resources and materials toward the recovery effort and had, in partnership with the Rudin Family and the ING Foundation, created a fund to aid New Yorkers impacted by the storm. They'd already raised over $2.6 million and asked recipients of their email to make a donation, all proceeds going to Hurricane Sandy Relief.

Sue and I watched the news throughout the day. Complete subdivisions had been flattened and fights were breaking out at gas stations, where people were desperate to get fuel for heating, as well as for their vehicles. We eventually headed out and stopped at a running store to gauge the feeling amongst the runners. Obviously, many were disappointed – thousands had travelled long distances and spent a lot of time and money investing in the race. Still, we didn't meet one runner who disagreed with the mayor's decision, but everyone agreed that he should have made it days earlier.

It became clear that our mode of transport would be Shanks's pony. Subway lines were limited and the buses and trains that were running were so overcrowded that the police had to provide crowd control.

We walked north on Third and then across Fifty-Ninth Street to Central Park. The mile markers were there, as were hundreds of people, just standing around the finish line. Here the mood was sombre. However, in other parts of the park, many people were out to enjoy the warm day. It was weird to see the hustle and bustle of the streets, shops and restaurants in this part of the city, knowing that other parts of the same city lay in ruins.

On the Sunday morning, a group of 170 Irish runners met in the lobby of our hotel, intending to go to Central Park for a run. Many wore their marathon shirts and race bibs. I decided to join them, as did many others. We walked to the park and headed off on a 10-kilometre loop. What I encountered was something I'll never forget: thousands of runners from all nations, some carrying flags or messages, had turned up to run. Many completed the full marathon distance. Sue joined the hundreds of supporters who had come out to cheer. The noise at times was deafening. The whole atmosphere reduced me to tears. I know you runners will get it when I talk about the spirit of running together for a cause – and we all had a cause. Afterward, we went to the south end of the park and donated money and clothing. This reminded me of the support I received during Marathon Quest 250.

We took a detour back to our hotel via Hell's Kitchen, where we strolled around the flea market. Sue and I talked about what we were going to do next and pondered whether or not there was a way to help out. Back at the hotel, I found a website that directed me to a location in Brooklyn where I could volunteer.

And so Monday morning found me setting out for Saint Jacobi Lutheran Church, in Brooklyn. The day before, Sue had used some eye drops and unfortunately had a bad reaction to them. Her eyes had closed over, and where the drops had run down her cheeks she looked like she had severe sunburn. I had to leave her at the hotel, rinsing her eyes.

At Grand Central Station the subway was jammed so I ran 28 blocks south to Union Station and jumped on the R Train to Fifty-Third Street. At the church, I entered the chapel and had a ten-minute orientation. The organizers were the Occupy Sandy group. These were the same individuals involved in Occupy Wall Street. They were looking for "runners" so I spent the day running up and down stairs, taking donated supplies from a basement and loading them into any vehicle that became available. Flashlights, batteries, baby food, diapers, pet food, clothing – the list was endless, and the organizers were constantly getting requests for more. I have to say, it was very well organized, but I did wonder where the Red Cross was. By the time I got back to the hotel, I was ready for a bath and a hot meal. Sue's eyes were much improved. We watched television coverage that showed us a stark contrast between Sandy's devastation and the hype and razzamatazz connected with the Obama and Romney presidential campaigns.

The next day we went home. It certainly wasn't the trip we'd expected, but it still resonates for both of us. We saw desperation and heartbreak, as well as kindness and generosity. But we also experienced something else, something we found frustrating, shocking and disappointing. On Sunday, as we were walking back to the hotel from Central Park, we decided to cut through Bloomingdale's to warm up. It was cold outside, and we'd donated our gloves and scarves. At the Marc Jacobs counter, two young women were trying to decide which of the $600+ purses they should buy; only a few kilometres away, people were trying to decide whether to eat what little they had for supper or save it for breakfast, and whether or not it was worth it to walk the hours it would take to get to a polling station the next day to vote for the leader of one of the richest countries on the planet.

As we drove down Big Hill into Cochrane, it was good to see the lights of the town. We were home and safe. But I was still thinking of the thousands of New Yorkers, still without power or a place to live, with their Thanksgiving only a couple of weeks away.

It would be a long, slow journey to achieve some semblance of normality, but when there's a need, people come together and help each other.

Now it was time for me to push forward and focus on my next challenge, Hockey Quest 500.

On Saturday, December 8, 2012, Sue and I went to the Markin MacPhail Centre at Canada Olympic Park and watched the World Championship Sledge Hockey game between Canada and the U.S.A. It was closely fought, but the States came out on top, 1–0. The effort these players put out was incredible, and they were a true inspiration to all the children watching them and cheering them on. I must say I was disappointed at the size of the crowd. Canada is a hockey-loving nation so the arena should have been packed. Afterward, we went down to see the team. I chatted with Billy Bridges, one of the Canadian players. Billy is a Right To Play Athlete Ambassador, a firm believer in sport for all. He went around chatting with kids, signing autographs and having his photo taken.

Hockey's a funny old game. I picked up my first hockey stick at the age of 22. I was living in Kimberley, BC, and was invited to join the men's recreational league. The only problem was I had never skated before. Well, that's not quite true. When I was 16 I had rented a pair of skates at a rink in England and spent 30 minutes walking around the side of the arena, clutching the boards. Despite this memory, I was not put off, and I bought some second-hand gear and headed out into the unknown. The players were very kind to me, and during the first season I spent more time on my butt than on the skates. I also had permanently bruised elbows and hips, but I persevered.

My hockey career took me from Kimberley to Yellowknife, where I played for the Dusters, a local teachers' team. My game slowly improved, and I found that my five-a-side soccer experience helped with my positional play. My final years of rec hockey were played in Sudbury, Ontario, where, every Sunday night, a group of us would get together for the Black Knights vs. White Knights. I didn't play again until 2010, when I got a call from the Rotary Relics in Cochrane and had my first experience in the Kimmett Cup.

After the sledge hockey game, I was excited to get back on my skates and get ready for the Kimmett Cup again, and Hockey Quest 500.

Sledge Hockey

Ice sledge hockey was invented at a rehabilitation centre in Stockholm, Sweden, during the early 1960s by a group of men that, despite physical impairment, wanted to continue playing hockey. The men modified a metal frame sled, or sledge, with two regular-sized ice-hockey-skate blades that allowed the puck to pass underneath. Once they had their sledges, the group used round poles with bike handles for sticks and played without any goaltenders on a lake south of Stockholm. The sport caught on and, by 1969, Stockholm had a five-team league that included both able-bodied and physically impaired players. That same year, Stockholm hosted the first international ice sledge hockey match between a local club team and one from Oslo, Norway.

Teams from Norway and Sweden played one another once or twice a year throughout the 1970s. Then, beginning with

Great Britain (1981), other nations began to form teams, including Canada (1982), U.S. (1990), and Estonia and Japan (1993). Two Swedish national teams played an exhibition match at the inaugural Örnsköldsvik 1976 Paralympic Winter Games in Sweden. But sledge hockey did not become an official Olympic sport until Lillehammer's 1994 Paralympic Winter Games. In Vancouver, BC's winter games (2010), the sport evolved again, when teams were permitted to have both male and female members.

EIGHT

Hockey Sticks and Tutus

"You miss 100% of the shots you don't take."
– WAYNE GRETZKY, hockey player, quoted in
the *New York Times*, 1996

Every year the Kimmett family and friends, Jason Baserman and Joe MacLellan, put on a huge pond-hockey tournament in Cochrane. In 2013 they were happy to add something special to the event: an attempt to set a Guinness World Record for the most number of players in a single hockey game: Hockey Quest 500. This would be Quest #6, and it would be a big one.

The start of January was busy. The *Calgary Herald* named me one of "20 Compelling Calgarians," and I spent a weekend at a south-end Chapters bookstore, talking about *Marathon Quest* and Right To Play. I spent those two days signing books and talking about

Marathon Quest and the Quests for Kids. I spoke to many people, among them Glenda Zamzow and her son Marcus. She had heard about the 250 marathons I had run and wanted to read my book. A week later, I received an email from her, saying: "I've been reading your book and it has really resonated with me...sports have changed my life as well. I saw a T-shirt at the Running Room and it said, 'Running, it's cheaper than therapy.' Loved it!...You have helped our family with your Marathon Quest, sports have helped me and my children, and we would like to 'pay it forward.'"

Glenda went on to say that, during 2013, she and her husband Richard and two sons, Derek and Marcus, wanted to do a number of events and fundraise for Right To Play. On January 13 I visited them and told them more about Right To Play and its programs around the world, working with disadvantaged children. We then brainstormed ideas for events that the family might attempt. One idea was for Marcus to do a 55-kilometre cross-country ski "Birkie." He also wanted to do a 5-kilometre race on a pogo stick. Derek wanted to do a 5-kilometre race on stilts. I was very impressed with other activities they planned to do, either individually or as a family. Their goal was to raise $25,000 for Right To Play and have lots of fun doing it.

Once in awhile, an event comes along that brings people together from diverse backgrounds, cultures and ages for a common goal. Hockey Quest 500 (HQ500) was such an event. The quest would be part of the Fifth Annual Kimmett Cup pond-hockey tournament in 2013. The tournament began in 2009 to raise money for the Lindsey Leigh Kimmett Foundation. Planning for HQ500 began right after the 2012 tournament, when Reid Kimmett suggested we combine the Kimmett Cup and the quest. We also agreed that all the fundraising from the tournament weekend would go to Right To Play, and we set a target of $400,000, with matching funds. This event would be an attempt to set a Guinness World Record for the most players in an exhibition game of hockey, a brand new record. Guinness had set a minimum of 75 players. In discussions with Reid, we decided to try and get 500 players to participate. Our thinking was that even if we fell a bit short in our target, we would still stand more than a good chance of setting the record.

Early on the morning of Saturday, January 19, Ciaran Dunn, Ginelle Polini and several other members of the University of Calgary Right To Play Club set up registration tables for the players. The puck was dropped at 8 a.m. at the Totem 2 ice surface, in the Spray Lake Sawmills Family Sports Centre, and the game was on. Each player had to play at least ten minutes and control the puck at least once. During the day, line after line went onto the ice. Following are profiles of some of the players.

Lau Mafuru: Lau is from Tanzania and only started skating two months before HQ500. Three weeks before the quest, Lau took a spill, splitting his lip and getting five stitches. Despite all that, Lau skated hard to become a Guinness World Record holder.

Charlie Masciangelo: Charlie is 12 years old and loves the Guinness World Record books. During the game, he played his ten minutes and scored three goals. Even better than that, he raised $701 for Right To Play and, with matching funds, this amount helped 56 kids.

Glenda and Derek Zamzow: Glenda and Derek completed their ten-minute shifts with gritty determination. For the rest of the day, they were fundraising and selling sumptuous goodies including cupcakes, crispy-rice squares and specialty chocolates to all the hockey players and friends milling about at the centre. By the end of the day, their Sweet Money Twisted Tortes sales had raised $365. This is the first of ten events the Zamzow family committed to in 2013. Their objective was to raise $25,000 for Right To Play.

At 5 p.m., nine hours after the start, the final whistle blew. In the end there were 374 players involved in HQ500. We didn't hit our 500-person target, but we had more than enough to set the new record. Ages of the players ranged from 5 to 65. Two players wore tutus, Kelly Kimmett and yours truly. Over the next couple of weeks, we hit our donation target, and we crossed our fingers as all the appropriate documentation was compiled and sent in to Guinness.

Hockey Spreads Joy in Eabametoong First Nation

Hockey isn't a gentle sport. In fact, injuries are a part of the game. But in Eabametoong First Nation, a remote community in northern Ontario, hockey heals. When the community lost a member one winter, the 1,300-person neighbourhood was hit hard. PLAY's Hockey for Development workshop was to take place the week following the tragedy, and it went ahead. Chief and council and PLAY Community Mentor Justin Morris knew Eabametoong's youth needed to get together around something positive.

Youth came out to the clinic in big numbers. John Chabot and Andrew Antsanen worked with 138 children and youth over the course of four days, helping them build hockey skills. The workshop ran in partnership with the school, so all the students got out on the ice to play every day. And the program brought in some youth who didn't attend school, giving both groups of youth a chance to play together and build connections. Girls and boys played together, and there was one "girls-only" ice time. The PLAY Program Officer for the community, Courtney Strutt, was proud to say, "Every set of skates we brought was on the ice!"

Quest #6: By the Numbers

Hockey Quest 500 (January 19, 2013)

Objective: To have 500 players in an exhibition game of hockey and set a Guinness World Record for largest number of players in a hockey game

Location: Spray Lake Sawmills Family Sports Centre, Cochrane, Alberta, Canada

Status: Guinness World Record set at 374 participants

Donations: $100,000

Matching funds: $300,000

Total: $400,000

Kids helped: 8,000

Funds application: Benin, West Africa

NINE

A Mountain to Climb

"It is not the mountain we conquer, but ourselves."
– PAUL STANLEY WARD, *Edmund Hillary:*
King of the World

We embarked on a trip of a lifetime to Kilimanjaro, Tanzania. Our friends Lau and Leesha had a baby girl, Oasis, and as her godparents, Sue and I were invited to her naming ceremony in Lau's home village of Mto wa Mbu, Tanzania. Add to this Quest #7: an attempt to run the Kilimanjaro Marathon and, three days later, climb the 5895-metre mountain, in 24 hours. Time to get training.

On February 23, 2013, I left for Tanzania. As I flew out of Calgary, I thought about how this trip came about. I had met Leesha and Lau Mafuru in 2011 at a Rotary meeting in Cochrane. Leesha's mom, Donna, is a member, and they were her guests, visiting from Edmonton. I sat next to Lau, and we hit it off right away. He is from Tanzania and has his own trekking company, Boma Africa. At the end of October 2011, Leesha and Lau had a baby girl, Oasis.

We were thrilled when they asked us to be her godparents. They also asked if we would go to Tanzania, in early 2013, for Oasis's naming ceremony. We then became known as Baba Mlezi and Mama Mlezi, which roughly translates from the Swahili as godfather and godmother.

During a trip to visit Lau and Leesha in Edmonton, Lau and I went for a run along the North Saskatchewan River. At the time, I was trying to get an idea for Quest #7 and during that one-hour jog we came up with a plan. Lau and I hoped to complete the Kilimanjaro Marathon on March 3 and, three days later, climb the highest mountain in Africa. Kilimanjaro Quest 95.2 – 42.2 kilometres for the marathon, and 53 kilometres up the mountain – was born. Instead of taking the usual five to seven days to climb the mountain, we would attempt to do it in 24 hours. Sue and I would also volunteer at a local orphanage.

Preparing for this quest was tough. I would put my treadmill on a steep incline or run up and down the hills of Horse Creek Road, near our home. Kilimanjaro's summit is at 5895 metres, while my house in Cochrane is at 1159 metres – that's a lot of altitude to account for. In the middle of February, to further enhance my training regime, I went for a hike with my friends Andrew Serle and Mike Kirby, planning to summit a local peak, Moose Mountain, which stands at 2437 metres. After hiking for five hours, we reached the saddle below the summit. We hit 2305 metres, but with dusk approaching, time was running out, and we had to turn back. What we accomplished was a tough pill to swallow. Our hiking that day didn't even equal half the height of Kilimanjaro. No matter, tomorrow was another day.

Sue headed out to Tanzania before me and spent a day in London visiting our son Calum and her sister Lynne, and then she joined me in Amsterdam for the final part of our outward journey. The KLM flight showed the Disney film *Brave*. I particularly connected with the line: "Whatever you want is within yourself, you just have to be brave enough to find it." It seemed a perfect mantra for me.

We arrived at Kilimanjaro International Airport on time, and as we stepped onto the tarmac, we were hit by a wave of warm air. It was a beautiful, clear night and the moon and the stars were out. There was a modest lineup at Immigration, but one of the officers noticed my Right To Play shirt and told us he knew of the organization. He said, "I know Right To Play, protecting the right of the child." He wasted no time in stamping our passports.

Lau was there to meet us and drive us to the Sarantoga Falls Lodge, on the outskirts of Arusha, where we would spend the first three nights of our stay. We drove for about 45 minutes and then turned down a side road. I use the term "road" loosely here: it was a rutted track Lau had to negotiate by slowing to a crawl. When we arrived at the lodge, we were greeted by the owner, Joyce. Even though it was well past 10 p.m., Joyce showed us to our accommodation – a round hut with a corrugated roof and sides covered by wooden slats. Our hut included a double bed, seating area and, sectioned off by a stone wall, a shower, washbasin and toilet. It was everything we could want for a truly comfortable stay. That same evening, she served us a three-course meal, beginning with a delicious, green-banana soup.

Joyce cooked our meals out in the open on a stone oven, and they were all very tasty. Included in the fare were the biggest avocadoes I've ever seen, plucked from local trees, as well as fresh, local pineapple, mango and tiny sweet bananas. We ate in the outdoor dining area, which was covered by a roof made of banana leaves and looked out over the lush, green valley below.

The next morning, Lau was due to come around at 6 a.m. and show me a route for my daily run. He arrived at 6:45 a.m. Sue and I soon came to learn that there is a thing called "Tanzania Time." As they say in Swahili, *hakuna matata*, no worries. Speaking of Swahili, my nickname amongst the locals came to be *Poli, Poli*, Slowly, Slowly – for obvious reasons. We ran for an hour that morning, and I got my first real glimpse of life in Tanzania. Children in uniforms were heading off to school, the little stores were already doing good business and the local people were friendly. Our run took us through the Mountain Meadows community. About halfway, we reached the hustle and bustle of one of Arusha's main roads. We turned back into the forest and found a beautiful single track that ran along a stream. When we came to a break in the trees, Lau told me to stop and look north. I did, and there it was, in the distance, the mighty Kilimanjaro.

Later that day, Lau picked us up in a Land Cruiser to take us on a mini-safari in Arusha National Park. On the way, we had to take some Italian tourists and a couple of guides to the park gates to meet up with a larger safari group. We had to stop in the city of Arusha to pick up some supplies and so the Italians decided to do some shopping and have lunch. In the meantime, Sue and I browsed around the shops in Arusha. We saw a little girl of about three who was helping her mom sell flowers. She was collecting the stalks as her mom cut them. Her dad was there, too, and he told us her name was Gladness. We had a game of peek-a-boo with her by hiding behind a tree. She was delightful.

Lau had to get the Italians to the park gate by a certain time in order for them to meet up with their group. But, due to them taking a long lunch and then forgetting their camera, we were late. The group had already left the park gates by the time we arrived. The Italians couldn't set off on their own, as they were required to have a rifle-packing park warden with them. Also, the porters, who were meant to carry the food for the trip, had left with the bigger group and, you guessed it, we had the food in the Land Cruiser. There was nothing to do but start the climb toward the safari's base camp in the vehicle and hope we would catch up with the group. The track was really rugged and steep.

One of the guides with us, Kidori, said that when you drive on one of these bumpy tracks it's called having an "African massage." Eventually, we met up with the group. It was already late afternoon and we were not far from the base camp, so we offered to drop off the supplies rather than make the porters carry them. They were very grateful. We continued along, but our journey to camp didn't go as planned. On a particularly steep part of the track, the engine stalled. Lau tried several times to get us going, but after a few attempts, it was obvious the battery was dead. The group of climbers passed us. Lau then tried to jump-start the vehicle by putting it in gear and letting it roll down the hill. This only resulted in it swerving backward into a ditch.

Lau tried to summon help on his cell phone, but the service was intermittent. By now, the light was beginning to fade and Lau became concerned. He told us he was worried about leopards, which caused Sue and me to worry, too. We decided we'd have to leave the vehicle and try to make it to base camp before dark. We'd be able to stay there until morning and then try again to summon help or leave the vehicle and make our way back down on foot. Just as we were gathering a few items to take with us, Lau said he could hear an engine in the distance. Suddenly, a large blue truck appeared out of nowhere. We couldn't believe our eyes, or our luck.

The driver told us his name was Amin, and he had to go a little farther to drop off some construction supplies, but he would come back and see if he could help us. True to his word, he returned about ten minutes later, without his load. Fortunately, he carried two batteries on his truck and gave us one of them. Talk about timing! We nicknamed him "Two-batteries Amin" and thanked him profusely.

We drove up to the camp, dropped off the supplies and made our way back down. By this time, the sun had almost disappeared and we'd missed out on our mini-safari. However, we were thrilled when two giraffes walked across the road in front of us, their silhouettes iconic against the evening sky.

On returning to the lodge, we realized that when the porters had unloaded the supplies at base camp, they'd accidentally unloaded Sue's backpack, too. We were too tired to worry about it and, besides, Joyce had prepared a wonderful meal of fish, rice, sweet potatoes and mixed vegetables, followed by a delicious dessert for which she told us she had a secret recipe.

The next morning, I expected Lau to join me for a run. However, Joyce let us know that Lau had called, apologizing because he couldn't make it but that his cousin, Brian, would join me instead.

Brian was sitting under a tree that Sue and I came to call the "Writing Tree" because we would often sit under it to write in our journals or enjoy reading a good book. Brian and I took a route through the village and backstreets of Arusha. We met lots of kids making their way to school. They were always pleased to see us running along and would call out, "Jambo," and give us high-fives. Brian explained that his mother was Lau's sister. He was 21 years old and was going to go to university to study business. He was also an Arsenal football club supporter, so we had a long chat about the issues the team was facing in the English Premier League.

Lau arrived at 11 a.m. with his good friend Samson, and we headed off to collect Sue's backpack, which had been brought down from base camp by one of the rangers. He dropped us at the Mount Meru Game Lodge, where we saw cranes, pelicans and a herd of zebra. We enjoyed a leisurely lunch, surrounded by beautiful flowering plants and some amazing trees. One of the women who worked there took us to what she called the "secret zoo," which was tucked away in another part of the grounds. There we saw a crocodile, turtles and porcupines.

That afternoon, Lau took us to the Moshono Foundation Children's Center at Moivaro Lodge. This is a local orphanage, run by Lau's friend Rose. At the time, it housed 12 children between the ages of 3 and 11. This was where Sue would be volunteering for a week, and I would help out when I could. Rose showed us around, and we met the six youngest children. The older ones were in school. The house had two bedrooms, one for girls and the other for the boys. There were not enough beds for everyone so they shared.

We played some games with the children, and they sang a song for us. Lau interpreted it – it was about God giving them food and good health, and they should thank Him for all the gifts. It brought tears to all our eyes. We told them we'd be back the next day to help them with their English lessons and play more games.

On arrival back at the lodge, we were relaxing in the dining area when big, dark clouds started to roll in. As we sat there reading, the winds came, along with the rain, sweeping into the dining space. We had to make a dash for Joyce's kitchen. It was only a very short distance, but we got soaked. The sound of the downpour was deafening, but there was something very exciting about being caught in the midst of it all. After about ten minutes, the rain ceased and we went to our hut to change into dry clothes. It was incredible to see the damage caused to the trees in such a short time; however, the sun soon came out and dried up the puddles.

Lau joined us for supper and we made plans for the next few days. Sue would be spending them at the orphanage, where I would join her for some of the time. She also had an afternoon booked at the Masai Market, where she would learn beading techniques from Masai women. Lau and I would take one day to tackle a 3000-metre peak, in preparation for our attempt on Kilimanjaro.

The next morning, we enjoyed our final breakfast at Joyce's lodge – we would be moving on to new accommodations at Lau and Leesha's Boma Africa House. Lau arrived with his friend Biggie, who would sometimes act as our driver. They dropped Sue and I off at the orphanage, where the little ones had already started their lessons with their teacher, Anna. They were learning to write and say their numbers in English. I sat next to 3-year-old Martha, and she showed me she was writing her numbers up to ten. Later on the children practised saying the names of colours.

It was all very formal. Sue had brought some beach balls with her from Cochrane. She blew them up, wrote the names of the colours on the different sections and invented a game to help the children learn. They had great fun, but we got the impression it was not formal enough for their teacher. I taught them a simple action number game before leaving them to eat their porridge lunch.

Later, on the way to Lau and Leesha's, we stopped at a store so that Sue could buy some coloured pencils and drawing books for the children. She had checked with the teacher to make sure this would be OK and was told that the children had never done any drawing, and the only pencils they had were kept for writing and math. We then made our way to a nearby food market, which covered a vast area and where you could buy every type of fruit and vegetable, as well as dried fish, live chickens, spices and fresh Kilimanjaro coffee. The sights and smells were amazing. It was hard to take it all in.

Leesha and Lau's Boma Africa House is on a large property. It's owned by the trekking company and reserved for guests who are either volunteering, climbing Kilimanjaro or, in some cases, both. At Joyce's lodge, the main problem we had to take in our stride had been infrequent power outages, but we came to learn that this is a general issue in Arusha.

The next day, after dropping Sue off at the orphanage, Lau and I set off for a training climb. We began by running along a rutted road, passing shops and a school on the way. At one point, Lau shouted for me to move aside and, as I did, two youngsters came hammering past us, towing loads of wood. Their mode of transport was like a bobsleigh, but pulled over gravel.

After an hour, we reached the top. There wasn't much up there, apart from a giant telecommunications tower. Going down was fun, slipping and sliding. By the time we reached the bottom, we were really sweaty and covered in dirt. We picked up a couple of Cokes at a little restaurant and then went to collect Sue.

As she climbed into the vehicle, we could see Sue was upset. She explained that she found it very difficult to watch the manner in which children were being taught. Having spent nearly 30 years as an elementary school teacher in England, Sue believes children should be encouraged to do their best and to be praised when they do so. However, as we had already noticed, teacher Anna was very strict. Anna became angry when the children made mistakes and, instead of demonstrating how to do what the child needed to learn, she just made them do the thing, erroneously, again and again. This method wasn't successful, and the children became even more upset – two of them had been reduced to tears. Bear in mind that the children were all between the ages of three and four, with Swahili as a first language. Nevertheless, all instruction given and their responses had to be in English.

The lessons consisted of writing numbers and letters over and over, and chanting them aloud, taking it in turns to point to them on a wall chart. The chart was so high up that the children would have to use a long stick to point, and the smaller ones had to do it standing on a chair. Three-year-old Shalom could hardly climb onto the chair. The children sat on dining chairs at a large table and only had about a ten-minute break to go outside into the courtyard. Apart from the beach balls Sue had given them the day before, they had nothing to play with, so Sue taught them a couple of singing games.

Lau explained that this was the way school was taught in Tanzania, but he agreed it wasn't good. There is such an emphasis on learning English, he explained. Sue understood that but suggested that there are ways of teaching that can make learning a positive experience. She hated it that these children were obviously scared to make a mistake and suffer the wrath of Miss Anna. I could tell she'd have liked nothing more than to go in there and teach them herself, employing practical activities, and make their learning a joyful experience. But all she could do was be a nurturing presence for the time she was with them.

Play Is Not a Luxury

Right To Play knows that play is not a luxury in many communities around the world. But play is every child's right, as Sue knows, and it can help kids young and old to learn, to feel connected and to feel comfortable within their communities. While we were exploring Arusha, Right To Play was helping 18-year-old Eradi Massawe, who, just a few kilometres east in Dar es Salaam, was working his magic as a Right To Play Coach at the MisMamo Youth Centre. Eradi was using his experience as an orphan born with HIV to help others, through play. Eradi teaches sport- and play-based activities to children aged 10 and younger. He knows a lot about the disease he lives with, and his confidence as an HIV-positive community leader is helping to change the stigma attached to youth like him.

Eradi, like the Community Mentors in Canadian Aboriginal communities, was reaching out to children, connecting with them and helping them to connect with one another. Play leads to learning, which builds confidence. Play = positive leadership.

Next we were off to the Masai Market, where Sue spent two hours with Calista, learning the beading technique used by Masai women. This would turn out to be a real highlight of the trip for her as she was doing a lot of beading at home, making jewellery to sell. Despite the language barrier, they had a great time. Sue used wire and tiny seed beads to create a coaster. By the end of the lesson, her fingers were sore from pulling the wire, but she was delighted with the product. The women thought it was funny to see this white woman trying so hard to do something they can do blindfolded. The tourists seemed a bit puzzled to see her there, on a tiny stool, beading with the local women. Sue bought some beautifully beaded boxes to take home, wondering how long it would have taken her to make one.

Meanwhile, Lau and I headed into town to get some chores done. We bought new showerheads, vegetables for supper and then we met up with Joyce and one of her guests, Triza from Nairobi, Kenya, who intended to run the Kilimanjaro Marathon and wanted to chat. She explained that she would be bringing runners down from Kenya for the event. She had seen Joyce's copy of *Marathon Quest* and wanted one for herself. I was happy to oblige.

It had been a long day, and we were all pleased to get back to the house, where one of the guys who worked for Lau helped me to get my laptop working and, after much-needed showers, we enjoyed a typical Tanzanian meal of ugali and mchicha, which Biggie told us we should eat with our fingers, so we did. It was delicious. Sue and I came to love mchicha, a green, leafy vegetable, similar to spinach.

Courtney, a midwife from Toronto, joined us at breakfast. Lau had picked her up from the airport late the previous night. She intended spending a month volunteering at the local hospital as part of a program that Leesha set up in conjunction with Canadian universities. Tanzania's infant mortality rate is 95 per 1,000, but the maternal mortality rate is a shocking 578 in 100,000, one of the highest in the world.

The next day, Sue and I both worked with the children at the orphanage. While there, I told Anna that I was attempting to climb Mount Kilimanjaro in one day and she got on her cell phone and called her friend Jackson to tell him about my quest. I then spoke to him and explained that first I would run the marathon. He told me I would die. Not exactly the encouragement I'd been hoping for, but I've come to realize that one just listens politely and then does what feels is right. After a few hours, Lau, Biggie and Courtney arrived to take us back to the house. We left the children playing with the beach balls.

Up until this time, Sue and I had spent very little time by ourselves. So we asked Lau to drop us off at a resort that is part of Mavoran Coffee Plantation, about a kilometre from the house. We enjoyed lunch by the pool and then spent the next few hours swimming and relaxing in loungers under the trees. It was especially luxurious for me, knowing that we would be heading to Moshi the next day for the marathon. We walked home through the village, and I spotted a lady at one of the communal water taps. She had two huge containers full of water. I indicated that I would carry them for her. She thought this was very funny but let me carry them to her house. Sue stopped at one of the little stores at the side of the road and bought some beautiful fabric.

On the way to Moshi, Lau made a detour. Up until then, the road had been good, but when we turned off, we found ourselves on what can only be described as the road to hell. It was so dusty that we couldn't have the AC on, so we were cooking inside the vehicle. We were bouncing around, over potholes, crazy bridges and volcanic rocks. One big bump threw Sue out of her seat. But, when we stopped and saw where we were, the destination was worth the discomfort. We found ourselves in an oasis surrounded by trees. There was a deep swimming hole, about the size of a large swimming pool, with over-hanging branches. Absolutely beautiful. Very soon, we'd all dived in and were enjoying the cool, clear water. The pool is fed by a river that passes over and is filtered by volcanic rock. It was hard work to swim against the flow – we soon learned to just relax and go with it. After this unexpected treat, we headed back out onto the road to Moshi.

When we arrived, the registration desk was still open. But I'd forgotten to bring the receipt for the payment I'd made online. I was told there was no proof of my registration and I would have to pay again. After a short discussion, I explained why I was running and gave the organizer my details. He gave me a number, then wished me luck and said he'd get TV media to cover what I was doing. Right To Play was certainly a respected organization in those parts. The RTP connection continued, too, when I met a women named Lindsay who was also registering to run and had previously raised money for the charity.

While we were standing in line, a young guy told Lau that he would love to run, but he didn't have the entrance fee. Could he help him out? Lau, always one to encourage youngsters, gave him the money and the guy disappeared. A hotel worker immediately approached and told us that the hard-up runner was operating a scam; some guys had been there all day, telling the same story and getting money from kind-hearted runners.

Lau disappeared, returning 15 minutes later with the guy, who was now holding a race number. Not only had Lau tracked him down but he had also made him use the money to register. He said he'd see him at the start line.

Lau took us to the lodge where we'd spend two nights. Sue and I had a lovely suite, and after we'd settled in, Lau took us to a great little outdoor restaurant where the kebabs were cooked over an open fire at the roadside. We tasted our first Tanzanian pizza. The pies were a bit different than the ones we're used to – covered with vegetables and egg – very tasty.

Later that evening, Lau set out to the airport to collect Leesha, her mother Donna, Oasis and two more Canadian midwives, Kirsten and Erin. Sue and I retired for a good night's sleep.

On race day, I slipped out into the open courtyard at 4:30 a.m. to prepare my water/CarboPro mix. Preparation is key to a successful marathon. I knew it was going to be hot, so I needed to hydrate and cover myself in +30 SPF sunblock. Millie, who works in the bar area of the hotel, dropped by to say I could get breakfast in the restaurant. Lau and I had agreed to meet at 5:15, but he wasn't yet there, by the time I was tucking into papaya, watermelon, avocado and bananas. This was followed by porridge and a boiled egg.

Lau finally arrived and at 5:35 a.m. we headed out, making one stop to pick up Lau's friends Kidori and Biggie. Biggie showed me one of the Kilimanjaro Quest 95.2 T-shirts he'd had printed, and it looked great.

We arrived at the stadium at 6:10 a.m. and the place was hopping. Runners were stretching and chatting. Slowly, the darkness lifted, and a beautiful sunrise announced the start of the day. In the distance, Mount Kilimanjaro could be seen, in all its majesty, its glaciers shimmering in the sunlight. At 6:25 the announcer called the runners to line up.

Lau suggested I go to the front for a "media shot." I wasn't too sure about this, but I went anyway. Around me were tall Kenyan and Tanzanian men and women. After the gun went off, we were away. Elbows and knees were flying, and I was swept along in a sea of bodies. Unfortunately, after about 100 metres down the cinder track, two runners fell in front of me and I tried to hurdle them. I didn't make it. I went sprawling in the dirt and several runners crashed into me as I tried to get up. I struggled back to my feet, and Lau, Kidori and I fell into a good pace. The kilometres clicked by. The route was an out and back eastward for 20 kilometres, then a westerly out and back for the remaining 22.2 kilometres.

We started the race in 20°C. At around the 16-kilometre mark, I was joined by Joseph, a young lad of about 12 years. He started running alongside me and chatted about how much he loved to run and that one day he was going to do the marathon. He stayed with me for about 10 kilometres and then headed off. We made the halfway point in 2 hours and 10 minutes. By this time, the temperature had reached 28°C.

The second half of the route took us up a steady incline for 11 kilometres. Lau was struggling with a knee problem. He stopped at a travelling medical aid van and they treated him with ibuprofen spray. Three kilometres later, I stopped at the same van and asked if they had some sunblock – unfortunately, they had none. I had put some on earlier but I knew I needed more. It was going to be a long final

15 kilometres. I struggled between kilometres 28 and 31. The heat was taking its toll, and at the aid stations, I downed cup after cup of Coke.

The route was lined with families enjoying the occasion, and dotted about were small wooden shacks, selling everything from baskets to beer. I was struck by the enthusiasm of the locals. Several were racing and had been charged a reduced entrance fee in order to encourage participation.

At 31 kilometres, we reached the turning point. What a change. The route was now downhill and the wind blew into my face. I suddenly felt strong and started to wheel it home. We had hoped to make it to the finish in 4 hours and 40 minutes, but the heat and the route had put the kibosh on that. I figured we would come in at around 5 hours. Lau's feet were hurting, and he wished he hadn't worn his Vibrams five-fingers shoes, but Kidori looked as fresh as a daisy. He was unfazed – simply amazing.

At last, we approached the stadium and could hear the beat of local music. The place was packed, and every runner was cheered across the line. The three of us finished together, at 5 hours and 23 seconds. Walking out of the finishers' chute, we were met by Sue, Leesha and little Oasis. We were given our medals and T-shirts. Post-race food was BBQ chicken and fries, cooked on an open fire, followed by a Kilimanjaro beer – excellent. It was a real party atmosphere.

Our merry gang walked back to the guest house under the shadow of the mountain. Part one of Kilimanjaro Quest 95.2 was complete. Lau, Kidori and I now had two days to rest before we tackled the second part, an attempt to summit the highest mountain in Africa in just 24 hrs. After a much-needed shower, I should have taken a nap, but my thirst got the better of me, and I returned to the courtyard for a beer.

Before heading out for supper, I put up a post on The Daily Mile website. It read: "Kilimanjaro Quest Part 1 completed. I will attempt Part 2, to climb the mountain, in 24 hours." Within four minutes, I received this response: "When will you post race report and photos?"

I thought, "There's no rest for the wicked."

The next day we made our way back to Arusha, and upon our arrival at Boma Africa House, we were greeted by Becca, who worked at Mount Royal University in Calgary. She had arrived after a gruelling 29-hour journey, via Addis Ababa. She was in Tanzania to finalize plans for some of her students to take part in the CIDA-funded midwifery program. Strangely, I had met Becca before – she had attended a presentation I had given in January at Mount Royal University in Calgary.

Sue and I decided to walk a kilometre to Modovia Lodge and enjoy a swim in the pool. It's a beautiful spot where you can just relax on a sunbed in the shade of the trees and enjoy being waited on by the excellent staff. We stayed there for four hours, swimming, eating lunch, drinking coffee, reading, listening to the birds and watching the butterflies. Again, for me, it was much-needed relaxation before the second stage of the Kilimanjaro Quest, which would begin bright and early the next morning.

That evening, as we ate a wonderful meal of chicken pilaf cooked by a local lady, my thoughts turned to the climb ahead of me, and I reminded myself to take my first dose of Diamox – a medication used to prevent the symptoms of altitude sickness – in the morning. Kilimanjaro Quest 95.2, part two, would soon be kicking into gear.

At noon the next day, I gave Sue a big hug, told her not to worry. and then Lau, Kidori and I set out. The drive to Moshi was another bone-cruncher. Along the way, we picked up porters Frank and Lala, as well as some trekking gear, a gas stove, pots and pans and hiking poles. Lau went into a climbing shop in Moshi and came out with a critical piece of gear: an oxygen bottle. Time was ticking, and by 4:30 p.m., we had to get to the Machame Gate, the entrance to one of the six routes up Mount Kilimanjaro. We got there at 4:40, but Lau said not to worry, "We're on Tanzanian time." Lau needed to buy a permit for our climb, so he headed into the office to talk to the warden. He came out 15 minutes later looking very worried. He said, "They told me the one-day permits have been banned. I don't think we can go

Altitude Sickness

Altitude sickness – or acute mountain sickness (AMS) – includes a series of symptoms occurring as effects of acute exposure to low partial pressure of oxygen at high altitudes, usually above 2400 metres. AMS is a collection of nonspecific symptoms, resembling a case of flu, carbon-monoxide poisoning or a hangover. It's hard to know who will be affected by altitude sickness, but most people can ascend to 2400 metres without difficulty. But some otherwise healthy people have experienced AMS at around 2000 metres above sea level. Symptoms include headache, fatigue, stomach illness, dizziness and sleep disturbance. Exertion aggravates these symptoms. AMS symptoms often manifest six to ten hours after ascent and generally subside in one to two days, but they occasionally develop into the more serious conditions. AMS can progress to high-altitude pulmonary edema (HAPE) or high-altitude cerebral edema (HACE), which are both potentially fatal.

up, but I'll see what I can do." He then turned around and headed back into the office. The next 30 minutes dragged by, and I was growing increasingly concerned. Was this the end of the quest? If so, what the heck was I going to do?

Lau came out smiling. The warden had contacted the park's chief warden and explained about the quest and the raising of funds for Right To Play. After more phone calls and discussion, he decided to give us special dispensation for our attempt. Also, that particular warden just happens to be an uncle of Lau's, which probably didn't do any harm. We all piled back into the van, relieved that the quest was still on.

We reached Kibosho Lodge at 7 p.m., just in time for supper. Over a meal of barbequed fish and rice, we chatted about the route. A couple of days before, Lau had dropped a bit of a bombshell. I thought we were taking the Marangu Route, also known as the "Coca-Cola" route – the oldest and most-established trail on the mountain. Lau said that I was mistaken; we would take the Umbwe Route. It really didn't bother me at the time, as I thought the routes would all be pretty similar.

However, I found a guide book on a table at the lodge, and I checked out what it said about Umbwe. "This short, steep route, possibly the most scenic of the lot, is not recommended as an ascent route as it is very steep in parts and involves one short stretch of genuine rock climbing." Turns out the Umbwe Route has the distinction of being known as the most challenging route on Kilimanjaro.

At 8 a.m. on Wednesday, March 6, I was sitting with Lau and Kidori, having my last breakfast before the ascent. Kibosho Lodge was a great place to spend the night before the push to the top. It is only

200 metres from the Umbwe Gate, where we would begin the ascent. Our six porters headed up Mweka, on the trail by which we would make our descent. They would wait for us at the Millennium Hut.

We had hoped to get away by 9 a.m., but signing park entry forms and personal risk waivers held us up. Lau, Kidori and I finally got away at 9:15. It was hard to believe we were starting on a 24-hour, 53-kilometre, 5895-metre adventure to the top of Africa.

On the way up the mountain, one ascends through five ecological zones: cultivated, tropical, moorland, desert and arctic. We quickly made our way through the first two. The path was good and we power walked most of the way, arriving at Umbwe Camp after three hours. If you're doing the five-day trip, this would be the campsite for Day One, but for us there was no stopping. The next zone, moorland, was amazing: bright green moss, skinny trees and old-man's beard hanging from branches. We spotted a colobus monkey perched high up in a tree. Lau told me that these primates have four fingers and that *colobus* means "cripple." The moorland had more challenging terrain than the previous two zones. One section involved proper rock climbing, nothing too difficult, but definitely not trekking.

Soon the trees and shrubs disappeared, and we entered the desert zone. After six hours of trekking, we arrived at Barranco Camp. There we met Rich and Tracey from Sheffield, England. They were having a great time and so far had been handling the altitude well. This camp is at 3962 metres. The highest I had previously been was 2438 metres. The temperature was dropping, so we changed into our cold-weather gear. Lau told us that we now had a seven-hour hike to the summit.

Events would prove otherwise.

We plodded through the desert zone and entered the arctic zone at around 6 p.m., just as darkness started to fall. We pulled on our headlights and geared up for the long climb ahead. The terrain was getting tougher and tougher, and by the time we reached Arrow Glacier Camp at 4999 metres, we were looking for a cup of tea. Lau visited three tents to see if he could get any. One guide asked if he had a "stolen permit" as we didn't have any camping gear. Lau explained that we were attempting to climb the mountain in 24 hours and raise funds for Right To Play. They didn't let him in.

In another tent, I found two Brits, Andrew, a surveyor, and Ashley, a project engineer. They both worked in London and had done this climb a number of times before. Ashley asked what I was doing. I told him about Marathon Quest 250, and he said I was "barking mad." They told us we should make Crater Camp in about four hours and that the summit was about an hour from there. They kindly provided us with plates of chicken pilaf and cups of tea. We then said goodbye and headed out into the freezing night.

We had definitely reached the arctic zone. Snow and ice skirted the trail, and the temperature had dropped to −15°C. I had a great headlight, Lau's was weak and Kidori didn't have one at all. The trail started to get more and more technical, and it seemed that Lau was having a hard time finding the route. I didn't have a headache or nausea, but my breathing was getting faster and heavier. I was using the Sportiiii, made by 4iiii in Cochrane. This device, mounted on my glasses, was feeding me visual and audible data about my pace and heart rate, which I was surprised to find never rose higher than 120 beats per minute.

We climbed on and on, tackling tricky rock faces covered in ice and snow. At one point, I was stuck on a steep scree slope, Kidori on one side and Lau on the other. It was getting ridiculous. I was actually happy that it was dark and I couldn't see more than a couple of metres in front of me. An unimpeded glimpse down the mountain would have scared the pants right off me. At another point, I rested, and, as I took off my CamelBak, my camera slipped off the belt and started to roll down the mountain. Instantly, Kidori was after it. I thought it was gone, but a few minutes later he appeared out of the darkness, camera in hand.

By 3 a.m. we had been climbing for six hours, since having left Arrow Glacier Camp. I was 5334 metres up Kilimanjaro and freezing. As the minutes and hours ticked by, I grew colder and more exhausted. Seven hours after leaving Ashley and Andrew, we arrived at Crater Camp. Lau looked at me and said, "You're not going to the summit." To be honest, I felt relieved. My lips had turned blue and I was shaking like a leaf. Lau visited a number of tents and found six porters and a guide, Lenard. When Lau told him what I was trying to do and why, he gave me a cup of hot chocolate. Then one of the porters cooked up some chicken and vegetable soup, and a third guy suggested I turn my back to the stove to warm up. Soon, my body was feeling toasty inside and out. I finished a cup of black, sugary coffee. I was feeling much better. I talked to Lau about the possibility of continuing on. He said he thought that now I could. Lenard and his porters were my "Kilimanjaro Angels" – without them I would never have had a chance to reach the top.

At 5:15 a.m. we left the friendly confines of the porters' tent and started the trek to the top. We had reached a point where other routes converge with Umbwe and were able to follow well-trodden footprints in the ice and snow. I was pretty well done. I had used just about my last reserves of energy, and my breathing was now so fast, I was panting. Every so often Kidori gave me a push to keep me going. As we passed the 5791-metre mark, the sun came up. It was an amazing blood-red and reflected off the huge glacier.

Lau pointed out the silhouette of the sign at the summit, 300 metres ahead, and at 6:15 a.m., after 21 hours of trekking, we reached Uhuru Peak, 5895 metres, the highest point on Kilimanjaro and Africa. I had taken a few items with me. The first was a huge Right To Play banner, second "Lammy the Lamb," a toy lamb that accompanied me on all my adventures and Right To Play's number-one supporter. The third item was a commemorative card for Lindsay Leigh Kimmett. Lindsay had climbed Kilimanjaro, and the mountain had meant a lot to her. After the requisite number of photos, it was time to head down. Lau, Kidori and I took the Mweka Route, the path home.

My stomach started to play up, and I was walking at a snail's pace. My only thought was, "Get me off this mountain." We reached Barafu Hut at 4980 metres, and Lau found my "Kilimanjaro Angels" again. Lenard and his porters gave me Imodium and Cipro, an antibiotic, but would not take any money for them. I took the Cipro. They also gave me a bowl of soup, and I asked if I could take a power nap in their tent. One of the porters found a foam mat, and I laid down. They put a puffy climbing jacket under my head, and Lau covered me in a Masai blanket. I went out like a light. Thirty minutes later, I was up and feeling much better. We said goodbye to our hosts and were on our way. Over the next two hours, we marched down to Millennium Camp and met up with our porters Frank and Lala. This route is pretty straightforward, and we made good time. The sleep and Cipro kicked butt. Literally.

At 6:15 p.m. we began the final push from Mweka Camp to Mweka Gate. Thunder and lightning followed us all the way down. I was struggling again. Lau and Kidori were in front of me, and it took all I had to put one foot in front of the other. My headlamp started to throw up crazy shapes, and I began seeing faces in the rocks on the path. I didn't mention this to Lau or Kidori at the time.

At 11:05 p.m. we reached our destination. Kilimanjaro Quest 95.2 was done. We had completed the trip in 37 hours, 50 minutes and 30 seconds; that's 24 hours in Tanzanian time. Benjamin, our driver, was there to greet us, and we headed off on the two-hour drive back to Arusha.

The next day, after a good night's sleep, I was ready for breakfast. I joined the others, who were already at the table, and recounted the many incidents of the Kilimanjaro climb. Lau then set up a video camera, and we watched a replay of the first stage of our journey. We talked about making a sort of miniseries, each day posting a video on Facebook that covered a stage of the marathon and the climb. Daz, a videographer and friend of Lau's, was keen and said he'd put together some two-minute clips over the course of the coming week.

The rest of the morning, Lau, Kidori, Biggie, Sue and I hung out, drinking coffee and eating chocolate cake, while the midwives made a visit to the local hospital. When they returned, we all packed overnight bags in preparation for our trip to Lau's hometown, Mto wa Mbu, 80 kilometres southwest of Arusha, for Oasis's naming ceremony. We were on the road by 3:15 p.m., and the drive would take almost three hours.

When we arrived at Lau's parents' house, we were greeted by all his family and several friends and neighbours. We were a bit late and the party was already in full swing. Everyone made a great fuss over us and, after being introduced, we were led into an open space with a porch, its roof made of banana leaves. Sue and I sat with Lau's parents at the head table, which was beautifully decorated with a white cloth and fresh flowers, and were given huge platefuls of food, cooked out in the open by Lau's sisters. We had a good chat with Lau's father, a teacher who speaks excellent English and has a great sense of humour. Lau later took us on a tour of his house, showing us where he slept as a child and telling us about some improvements he wanted to make to the property. After wishing everyone goodnight, Lau drove Sue and me to a guest house, where we would spend our last night in Tanzania.

The next day, we wandered around the village of Mto wa Mbu. We visited the market and then spoke to a group of carvers, who were working in the banana plantation, and we enjoyed a glass of banana beer. Later that evening, Lau drove us to Kilimanjaro Airport. When we had originally talked to Lau about going to Africa, he said to Sue, "When you leave Tanzania, you will cry." At the time, Sue wasn't convinced. In fact, she wasn't that keen on going and really only agreed to the trip because she wanted to go to Oasis's naming ceremony. However, as we reluctantly said our goodbyes to Lau, she did become a little tearful and told him how very glad she was that she had made the trip. I know she fell in love with the country and the people we met, especially the children. There's something about the places in Africa we've visited that really got into our souls.

As we boarded our flight and headed to Amsterdam, we talked

about all the wonderful experiences we shared and the sights, sounds and colours. Amsterdam was where Sue and I parted ways. She boarded a plane to Heathrow to spend some time with her family, and I caught a flight to Calgary. During the trip I reflected on KQ95.2. No question it had been the most dangerous of the quests so far, and I almost hadn't made it. There is a fine line between success and failure and, to be honest, the final outcome often is in the hands of the gods. In the end, I had survived the altitude and made it to the top.

Quest #7: By the Numbers

Kilimanjaro Quest 95.2 (March 3–7, 2013)

Objective: To run the Kilimanjaro Marathon (42.2 kilometres) then climb to the summit and back in 24 hours

Location: Kilimanjaro, Tanzania

Status: Completed marathon in 5 hours and 23 seconds, summited in 21 hours and returned to base for a total time of 37 hours, 50 minutes and 30 seconds

Donations: $5,242

Matching funds: $15,726

Total: $20,968

Kids helped: 419

Funds application: Benin, West Africa

TEN

When in Rome

"I may not have gone where I intended to go, but
I think I have ended up where I needed to be."
– DOUGLAS ADAMS, *The Long Dark Tea-Time of the Soul*

*Upon my return from Tanzania, advanced planning for Quest #8
began in earnest. This would be a big one: TransRockies Quest 888.
Before the quest could begin, though, Sue and I took a spring holiday
in Rome, then headed over to London to run the Virgin London
Marathon. While in England, I also started planning ahead for
Quest #9 when I spoke with Rotary friends about a possible traverse
of the South West Coast Path. For fun, upon return to Alberta, I
attempted to set a GWR for the fastest marathon in full lacrosse
gear.*

On March 18 I got back into the swing of things by meeting Elijah Thompson at the Kyle Shewfelt gym festival. Elijah had sent me a message on Facebook, excited to meet me:

> Dear Martin, I was trying to find you! I am 11 and I've been raising money for Right To Play for 2 years. Maybe we can do something together soon…

Elijah's story blew me away. Elijah is a keen gymnast and had competed in Kyle Shewfelt's 2011 gym festival. Soon after the event, he sent Kyle this email:

> I am shy to start a fundraiser or something public like that, so I came up with this idea: I am working on ten circles on one-handle-long pommel for my Argo routines. Starting after KSGF, every training day that I made ten circles in a row in a turn, I earned one loonie for Right To Play from Mom. Then, in June that exercise got easier for me, so my coach, Miguel, switched me from ten uphill loops (Argo B Day 1 Pommel Horse Routine) to ten downhill loops on the pommel (Argo B Day 2 Pommel Horse Routine)…that was harder so I really had to work for a loonie at all. Some training days I got no loonies, some days I got two, one day I got three!! Now, I was closer to my goal of $100.00 for Right To Play, but I still was short. Miguel started me on two-handle big boy pommel with a block to start from. I was only getting three to five circles, but mom said if I got ten there, that would be another loonie. So…wait for it…I started getting ten on the big two-handle pommel!! More loonies!

Just like my downhill loops, some training days I earned no loonies, but some I got one, or two! Each time I put them in my green cup on my trophy shelf in my room. This is where I put medals, but also rocks and stones Mom gives me every time I learn a new skill. When I got ten of those, Mom would trade me for a $10.00 bill. I finally had ten, $10.00 bills. Now it was time to mail you [a] package with the special thing I made for you from my first Nationals, and I had enough for Mom to send you a full $100.00 for Right To Play!!

Right To Play means a lot to me. We have four kids in our family who all get to do sports. We also have three foster children around the world in very poor areas who don't get those chances. Last Christmas we sent them sports equipment through World Vision. Now I can help more kids through Right To Play. Please let me know the kinds of things my loonies will help kids to do.

Elijah continued to fundraise for Right To Play, and on February 26, 2013, he was awarded the Queen Elizabeth II Diamond Jubilee medal. When I met Elijah and his mom, Krista, at the festival, we had a great chat.

Later in the week, I completed my final long run before starting to taper off in advance of the London Marathon on April 21. But before London, Sue and I were going to Rome.

Sue had always wanted to visit Italy, Rome in particular. I decided to surprise her and booked a trip for us as part of her 60th birthday gift. We checked into the Hotel Royale Splendide, and "splendide" it certainly was. Refurbished in the Baroque style, it was sumptuous and ornate. The building had previously been a college, owned by the Catholic Church, which still owns the property.

We soon got ourselves organized, finding a great little underground supermarket on the way to the metro. We bought fruit, rolls, salad, cheese and cold meats, along with paper plates and bowls, serviettes, plastic cutlery and glasses, and, of course, a great red wine, all for about $23. We then headed off to Villa Borghese Park, Rome's "Central Park," which was at the end of the street, for a picnic. It was beautiful: lawns, statues, a zoo, museums and a lake. While sitting on a bench, enjoying pistachio gelatos, we spotted a number of runners, and Sue suggested that, one morning, I run a circuit of the park.

All through the parks and dotted about along the streets were beautiful old fountains. We noticed several people filling their water bottles or drinking straight from them. So I gave it a go. The water was cold and refreshing. After supper, we spent the evening drinking wine and planning. There was so much we wanted to see.

We acquired a map and directions from the hotel receptionist and made our way to the Trevi Fountain. We had great fun winding our way through the narrow backstreets, checking out the shops and cafés. At the fountain, we joined many other tourists, all vying for the perfect spot for a photo. We sat on a wall and took it all in, enjoying the glorious sunshine. On the way back we got slightly lost, but we found a great little café, where we enjoyed our first taste of real Italian coffee.

St. Peter's Square and the Vatican were on our list of places to visit. The next day, we made our way along the Tiber and were surprised at how brown and silty the water was. As we neared the

Pope Francis Believes in the Power of Play

In 2016 Pope Francis congratulated West Bank teacher, Hanan Al Hroub, upon winning the Global Teacher Prize. He said, "I would like to congratulate the teacher Hanan Al Hroub for winning this prestigious prize due to the importance she gives to the role of play in a child's education...A child has the right to play. Part of education is to teach children how to play, because you learn how to be social though games, and you learn the joy of life."

The Pope understands the power of play in a child's life. The power of play to enhance education and teach critical life skills is exactly what Right To Play has been working on around the world since 2000. Using a unique methodology guided by Right To Play Coaches, kids enrolled in RTP programs not only learn how to be social and joyful but also how to take care of themselves and how to be peaceful agents of change in their communities.

Here's how it works:

1. A child joins a Right To Play program with limited awareness of his or her behaviour, or potential.

2. Coaches lead regular games and activities that teach important lessons relevant to the child's life and community. Through play and Coach-guided discussions, the child comes to understand and be passionate about the education-, health- and peacebuilding-based messages he or she has learned and experienced.

3. Engaged in the program, the child begins to practise the lessons he or she has learned at home with family, friends and within the communities.

4. The child remembers Right To Play teachings and maintains his or her new and proactive behaviours.

5. The child becomes an advocate for his or her newly learned behaviours, teaching and sharing with others.

In Canada, PLAY programs function in the same way with Community Mentors in Aboriginal communities. As Right To Play Founder Johann Koss said in 2013, "We believe centre of the city, the pathways were lined with stalls and cafés, and there were street artists in abundance. We stopped for a cappuccino and studied our map, not much farther to go.

Finally, we were strolling up the Via della Conciliazione and entering Saint Peter's Square. We took in the atmosphere. Here we were, where, only a few weeks before, Pope Francis had been named the new head of the Catholic Church. We ate our picnic lunch and drank Chianti, perched on the base of one of the huge pillars that surround the square.

In the Sistine Chapel, seeing the magnificence of Michelangelo's fresco covering the ceiling, and his *Last Judgement* over the altar, was one of the highlights of our visit. We were lucky with our timing, as we missed the lineups. We were told it would be possible to get tickets for the audience with the Pope on Wednesday morning, so we decided we'd return.

The next morning, I headed out for an early run and found a new route around the perimeter of the park that led me to a great view in all directions. I could easily spot Saint Peter's Basilica, in the distance. Later in the day, Sue and I found the Villa Medici, ate gelato and admired the numerous statues dotted around and lining some of the pathways. The sun was shining, and we walked for hours.

The following day we took it easy, picnicking, relaxing, reading and running, before donning our tourists' hats and taking the

Top: Netball Quest 61 at the South Fish Creek Recreation Complex in Calgary. Below: Team photo, Netball Quest 61.

Top: Theo Two the Tug moored in Halifax harbour, Nova Scotia. Below: Peggy's Cove, Nova Scotia.

Top, left: Collecting pennies on Canada Day in Redwood Meadows.
Top, right: Poster promoting Lacrosse Quest 24. Below: Celebrating
the end of Lacrosse Quest 24.

Top: The Right To Play booth at the TSN Kraft Celebration Tour.
Below: Dianne Kimmett holds the $25,000 cheque from the TSN Kraft
Celebration Tour.

Top: Celebrating the completion of Cook Island Quest 100. Below: Teams receive confirmation of achieving the Guinness World Record for Soccer Quest 24.

Top: From left to right, Prime Minister Stephen Harper, me and MP Blake Richards at the Queen Elizabeth II Diamond Jubilee medal ceremony. Below: Scoring a goal in my pink tutu during Hockey Quest 500.

Top: The children at an orphanage in Arusha, Tanzania. Below: On the summit of Kilimanjaro with Lau and Kidori.

Top: Elijah Thompson at the Kyle Shewfelt Gymnastics Festival. Below: Running across Tower Bridge during the 2013 London Marathon.

Top: Flood damage in High River, Alberta. Below: At the start of
TransRockies Quest 888.

Top: Glenda, Derek and Richard Zamzow on the TransRockies Heli-Run.
Below: Tough going up Jacob's Ladder during TransRockies Moab.

154

Top: The Yukon Ultra with Paul (Turbo) Trebilock and Simon Donato from TV's Boundless. Below: The south Cornish coastline from the cliffs of the Minak Theatre.

Top: The "Questmobile" is unveiled at Cochrane Toyota. Below: Love Clap at McGill University, Montreal.

Top: Ball Hockey Guinness World Record attempt at Dublin Heights School, Toronto. Below: Players at the Abony Family Tennis Centre in Fredericton.

Top: Grandchildren Autumn and Nathan test out the tent on the "Questmobile." Below: Young runners at the December 31, 2014, year-end event.

Top: Sue becomes a Canadian citizen. Below: Children enjoying the Sue and Martin Parnell playground in the village of Mto wa Mbu, Tanzania.

Top: Dr. Suresh Subramaniam, neuro-ophthalmologist, at Rockyview Hospital, Calgary. Below: Captain Clot-Buster completes the 2015 Calgary Marathon.

subway to the Colosseum. As we stepped out of the subway station, the Colosseum was right there in front of us. A magnificent sight. We toured the area, soaking in the history, then we walked up a side path and visited a beautiful little church before making our way up onto a grassy area to eat lunch.

On our final full day in Rome, we headed back to the Vatican to pick up tickets to attend the Papal Audience. We couldn't believe how lucky we were to have the opportunity to see the Pope in person. When we reached Saint Peter's Square, we headed for "the bronze door," at which we had to queue in order to get our tickets. We joined a lineup of about ten people and got chatting with Patrick. He was from County Mayo, Ireland, and was travelling with his sister. She had gone sightseeing and had left him to wait for tickets. While waiting, the lineup grew considerably, and several people tried to jump the queue, including a couple of priests, but they were all put firmly in their places by an elderly nun who told them, in no uncertain terms, where they could find the back of the line.

Eventually, the door opened, and we made our way to a little office where we were given our passes. We then headed to the Basilica. It's very hard to describe the splendour and grandeur of the place. It truly is incredible. We wandered around in a state of awe. We entered a tiny chapel, where we sat, for a few minutes, in silent prayer.

My mum was a devout Catholic, and every Sunday she would take me, my two brothers and three sisters to church at Buckfast Abbey. My dad wasn't Catholic. However, he was the local butcher and supplied meat to the abbey and was great friends with the monks and fathers who lived there. The abbey has a gift shop, and one of its bestselling products is Buckfast Abbey tonic wine or, as the locals call it, "Bucky." The base wine comes in from Spain or France and then the monks add their "secret ingredients" to make it into a tonic. I remember many a Saturday going with Dad to the abbey and sitting next to the wine vats, chatting with Father Paulinus and Brother Bead about cricket, football and the state of the economy. The men would be enjoying a glass of "Heretic," the name they gave the wine before the "secret ingredients" were added, and I would have an apple cider. Those days are gone, but they are wonderful memories and they were with me as I sat in the chapel that day in Vatican City.

We had an early start to our last day in Rome and made our way to the Papal Audience. We soon got caught up in the throngs of people moving toward Saint Peter's Square. Once you get there, despite having tickets, it's very much first come, first served, as far as the seats go. The problem is there aren't enough seats to accommodate the number of tickets distributed. Sue and I found ourselves

Buckfast Abbey

Buckfast Abbey forms part of an active Benedictine monastery at Buckfast, near Buckfastleigh, Devon, England. Buckfast first hosted a Benedictine abbey in 1018, followed by a Cistercian abbey, which was built in 1134 on the site of the abbey that exists today. This monastery was dissolved in 1539 – the buildings were stripped and left as ruins, later to become a quarry. The stones rose again to become a Gothic mansion.

French Benedictine monks purchased the site in 1882, and they refounded a monastery dedicated to Saint Mary. The Gothic house became one of the monastic buildings. The church, mostly built on the same site as the former Cistercian church, was finally consecrated in 1932 but not completed until 1938.

The Benedictine abbey still exists today.

standing, which wasn't an issue, as it meant we could find a good spot to view the proceedings. There were approximately two thousand people there, all eagerly awaiting the appearance of the Holy Father. As we waited, an announcer called out the names of various groups that had made the pilgrimage, and as they were named, each group gave a rousing cheer. Suddenly, an enormous shout went up, and there was Pope Francis in his open-topped popemobile, which slowly took him along and across the aisles of people. We were moved to see how he interacted with the crowd, smiling and waving all along the route, scooping up children for hugs or leaning over to ruffle their hair. As he approached us, it was easy to get a photo. I couldn't believe how close he came to us. I thought about my mum, and how she would have loved this experience.

From the stage, the Pope addressed the crowd in Latin, and then we listened as his words were translated into various languages. His theme was "charity to others." Afterward, there was a choir and a musical performance from a visiting school. Too soon, Sue and I had to head to the airport and bid a reluctant farewell to Rome – but not before one last gelato, a ride on a two-seater tricycle and a final stroll around the Villa Borghese.

At Heathrow airport, we were met by Sue's sister, Lynne, and driven to her home in Petersfield, Hampshire. Sue loves this market town, with its quaint old buildings, market square, pubs and coffee shops, all within short walking distance from Lynne's house. I wanted to find a route for my morning runs, and Lynne suggested I check out the pathway around the pond on Petersfield Heath, which covers 36 hectares and is the site of a cluster of 21 Bronze Age barrows, or burial mounds. During the Middle Ages, the heath was common land, used for grazing livestock. In 1890 the land was developed as a golf course. Fairways were laid out and a club house built. In 1998, however, the golf club relocated and the land is now being returned to its original state. The pond is in the heath's west corner, encircled by a well-maintained pathway.

On my first run, I did one loop around the pond and then headed off into the heath. The going was quite tough, as England had just experienced one of its wettest springs and the ground was water-logged. I completed my run and headed into town, where I grabbed a copy of the local newspaper, the *Petersfield Post*, and settled into a coffee shop to read about life in this idyllic little community. The first couple of articles told me about a taxi driver being given a parking ticket and calling it "absurd." Then it was on to the more important issues of the day, "Court Orders Gypsies to Move On," "Blood Trail Linked to Window Smash" and, even more alarming, "Fireball in Sky above Town." Maybe not so idyllic, more like something from the Stephen Pegg and Edgar Wright movie, *Hot Fuzz*.

Later, Lynne drove us to another town, Chichester. After visiting the cathedral, we wandered around in the sunshine, exploring the shops and alleyways. The next day, Lynne drove us up to Calum's home in Wimbledon, London. On the first evening, we took the underground train to Canada House in Trafalgar Square. We had been invited by Don Gorman, my publisher at Rocky Mountain Books, to a literary event for Canadian publishers and writers. It was great to see Don again. We also met some other interesting people, including a man who is the Canadian distributor for the *Beano* and *Dandy* comics, my childhood favourites.

The next morning, Sue and I had breakfast with some old friends of mine, Stephen and Carol Lay. I had become friends with Stephen during my time at the Camborne School of Mines and had recently reconnected with him through Rotary. After catching up on our most recent news, we chatted about my idea for Quest #9: Rotary Coastal Quest 630 (RCQ630). I told him that I would be attempting to run and walk the South West Coast Path from Minehead, in Somerset, to Poole, Dorset, a distance of 630 miles (1014 km). The route took in the pathways, beaches, estuaries and cliffs of the southwest peninsula of England. Rotary chapters along the route would prove to be indispensable in my quest.

After lunch, Stephen and I agreed to meet up the following day and visit the Right To Play office in central London. Stephen wanted me to speak to his Rotary Club chapter in March 2014, and I figured he would benefit from finding out more about RTP.

Later in the day, Calum introduced me to his friend, Stephen Trumble. Stephen and his twin brother, David, are both talented artists who studied film at university with Calum. Some months before, their film company, The Flock of Condors, had been crowdsourcing for a film project and offering perks to those who donated. My perk was a storyboard, drawn by Stephen, based on *Marathon Quest*. I now wanted to talk to him about developing it into a graphic novel. We discussed the basic layout, and he shared some of his ideas, all of which were brilliant. Having already seen some of his work, I couldn't wait to see the end result.

The next day, we heard that two bombs had been detonated among spectators close to the finish line of the Boston Marathon.

The news coverage from Boston was, of course, shocking. I have run Boston three times and, if I hadn't been running the London

Marathon, I would have been there. The bombs had gone off three hours after the elite runners had finished, so they would have just about coincided with my finish time, and Sue would have been waiting for me as I came in. We were both in tears as we watched the horrific footage, both in sympathy for those affected at the scene and because it could have been us there, at precisely that horrible moment.

Later in the morning, I was still in shock when Stephen and I headed out to meet with Kathryn and Phil at the Right To Play office. They were both enthusiastic about my plan for Rotary Coastal Quest 630, and we talked long enough to fill in some of the details. The quest was starting to take shape. When Stephen left, I chatted with other RTP employees, with whom I would be running the London Marathon as part of the Right To Play team. The topic of the Boston bombings came up a number of times, but we were all determined to carry on with our plans.

Boston stayed with me all day, especially when I received a call from CBC Calgary, asking me to chat with Doug Dirks on *The Homestretch* about my response to the Boston bombings, and whether or not I was concerned about security for the London Marathon.

There was speculation about the status of the London Marathon. Should it be cancelled or postponed? The consensus was overwhelming: it would go ahead. Also, the organizers were donating two pounds for every runner toward the "One Boston Fund."

An article in the *Daily Mail* noted that before the marathon began, runners and spectators would observe a 30-second silence, in tribute to victims in Boston. To show solidarity, runners were encouraged to wear black ribbons. London police would provide extra security.

Race director Hugh Brasher said, "We want to show our support for our friends and colleagues in Boston at this difficult time for the global running community. We are determined to deliver an amazing event that will focus on one of the core pillars of the London Marathon, which is 'to have fun and provide some happiness and a sense of achievement in a troubled world.'"

I went to the race expo to pick up my race number and timing chip and then hopped on a bus and toured the race route. As I was chatting with other runners, I definitely picked up on a feeling of apprehension among the participants, but this was coupled with strong resolve for the race to go ahead.

Later in the day, Calum took us to the hotel where we would spend the next few nights. Over supper, we heard that the two suspected Boston bombers had been caught. This was good news and brought some element of relief. However, it made me realize how fragile life is, how

London Marathon

The London Marathon was founded by the former Olympic champion and journalist Chris Brasher and athlete John Disley. The first race was held on March 29, 1981: 6,747 runners were accepted for the race and 6,255 crossed the finish line on Constitution Hill. It is set over a largely flat course around the River Thames, and it begins in three separate points around Blackheath and finishes in the Mall alongside St. James's Park. It has become one of the top five international marathons run over the distance of 26 miles and 385 yards, which is the IAAF standard for the marathon established in 1921. And it is a large, celebratory, sporting festival that has raised over £450 million for charity since 1981, and holds the Guinness World Record as the largest annual fundraising event in the world.

there are elements in the world that want to crush the human spirit. For me, the answer to this disease is to not put your life on hold and cower. I thought about why running this marathon was important, and I realized that my desire for the London Marathon to proceed was not so much about wanting to run the race but about being part of a community, a bringing together of people for a common goal.

It made me think about Right To Play's peacebuilding initiatives. As Right To Play suggests in the article "Peaceful Communities" (on its website):

> One billion children in our world live in conflict-affected areas. In volatile areas, our programs encourage all children – regardless of the ethnic, cultural or historical divides they've inherited – to come together on neutral grounds and play.
>
> A game of Protector Dodgeball is not about hitting the opponent – it's about protecting your team. A game of Volley Tennis is less about scoring points than it is about the communication it takes to keep the ball in the air and get it over the net. After a game is over, our Coaches get the players talking about the importance of strong leadership and communications skills. This gets them thinking about how the skills they've learned can be used to make their communities better.
>
> For many children, conflict has not only torn them from their homes, but has made new neighbours of old enemies. Bringing kids together to play – whether on a football field or in a classroom – is an opportunity to foster the friendships and understanding that lasting peace is built upon.

This marathon had a slightly later start than I'm used to, but that was OK. It meant more time for breakfast before we had to head out. All the trains to Waterloo and Greenwich were packed with thousands of runners. I met two, Pam and Georgie, from South Africa, who had run the Comrades Marathon when I did.

At Greenwich we were directed to starting areas, based on our bib colours.

At 9:50 a.m. I was waiting with thousands of others in corral number eight. At 9:59 we all observed 30 seconds of silence, in remembrance of those who had been affected by events at the Boston Marathon, now one week ago. It was an unbelievable moment – there were over 36,000 people present and you could have heard a pin drop.

Then we were off. I thoroughly enjoyed my run through the streets of London, passing such great landmarks as the Cutty Sark, Tower Bridge, the Houses of Parliament and Canary Wharf. The one thing I wasn't used to and found somewhat strange was that there wasn't one moment when I had any space around me. There were just so many runners, many of whom were in costume. I saw Superman, a giant hand, ladybugs and Raggedy Anne. I spotted a man in a chicken suit, a two-person Jamaican bobsleigh, a rhinoceros, Wolverine and Mary Poppins. These runners were all raising money for causes close to their hearts.

I remember one runner in particular, but not because of a costume. I caught sight of her briefly, a girl, aged about 14, running on her own and wearing a sign that read "In Memory of My Dad." I was immediately reminded that we all have our own reasons for running, including personal goals, to raise funds for a great cause or simply to remember someone. I was running for Right To Play, but I'd like to think my sister Jan was running alongside me that day, too.

As the miles clicked by, I thought I might call Calum at the finish. He'd said he would try and watch the race from somewhere along the route. There were so many people lining the road, though, so I didn't really hold out much hope of finding him. Then, at the 40-kilometre mark, there he was, cheering and waving.

I was pipped at the post by Mary Poppins but was pleased with my time of 4 hours, 37 minutes and 51 seconds.

Back in Alberta, I started May with a bang as I began the first event in Quest #8, TransRockies Quest 888 (TRQ888). My objective was to complete 888 race kilometres over the course of ten events, from May to October 2013. During TRQ888, I hoped to raise $25,000 and, with matching donations of $3 for every $1, top out with $100,000.

In December 2011 I met Aaron McConnell, co-owner of Trans-Rockies when I was part of a committee for the Rotary Club of Cochrane that was organizing Run in the Park, an event to be held at the Glenbow Ranch Provisional Park. TransRockies had been retained to be the race organizers, and I was impressed by their professionalism.

In March of 2012, I was trying to come up with an idea for Quest #8. Previously, Aaron had told me that TransRockies held between six and eight events a year, including trail and road running, and mountain and road cycling. As I racked my brain for ideas, I hit upon the possibility of teaming up with TransRockies. I suggested to Aaron that, for Quest #8, I would attempt to complete all the events he had planned for 2013. We added up the kilometres that I would have to cover and it came to 888. Hence, TransRockies Quest 888 was born. Aaron loved it.

And so it was that at 6:03 p.m. on May 2, 2013, I was there when Aaron blew the whistle and a group of "Chasers" headed west from East Village Plaza in Calgary, along a path by the Bow River. Three minutes earlier a much larger group of "Skirts" had headed off in the same direction. This was the Skirt Chaser 5K, the first event in TRQ888. It had stirred up some controversy even before the whistle blew. There were comments on Twitter and Facebook expressing the opinion that the race was sexist and demeaning to women; even CBC got in on the act.

I asked Sue what she thought, and she said the negative comments were a load of nonsense, that it was just a bit of fun and people should lighten up. I asked her how I should pace myself for the race, and she told me to run as fast as I could but treat it like a fishing trip: catch and release.

I had arrived early at East Village Plaza and met up with Aaron and Jonathan McLeod, manager of marketing and communications for TransRockies. They said that the media had been buzzing around earlier but had headed off before the start. Aaron mentioned that 160 individuals had signed up, and of these 120 were women. I was in the "Chasers" group and ran one of my fastest five kilometres in years. Five kilometres down, 883 to go. Around the finishing area, everyone was laughing and joking and having a great time.

Before my next TransRockies event, I had a marathon to run.

At 6:45 a.m. on May 26, it was sunny in Calgary. This was great for approximately 13,000 runners who were there to take part in the 49th Scotiabank Calgary Marathon. But the heat would not be ideal for me. I was hoping to set a Guinness World Record for the fastest marathon in full lacrosse gear, including the helmet, shoulder pads, kidney guard, gloves and stick, and carrying a ball. I had been in training for the previous month. This was not a quest but a personal challenge. Despite this being a new record attempt, the administrators at Guinness had set me a sub-four-hour target so I knew this marathon would not be a walk in the park.

With me at the start line were Blaine Penny and his MitoCanada team. They were going for a Guinness World Record, too, for the fastest marathon with ten runners all linked together. They had to run sub-two hours and 57 minutes. Blaine and his team were raising money for MitoCanada, which was formed in 2009 by a group of mitochondrial disease patients, and their families and friends, with support from medical professionals. MitoCanada exists to provide support and practical information that helps to improve the quality of life and sense of community for patients and their families.

To have my record verified by Guinness, I had to have my whole run videoed, so Evan Weselake was my cameraman. He stayed behind me, riding a mountain bike the whole time with a GoPro camera strapped to the handlebars.

I was already feeling the heat when Calgary's Mayor Nenshi started the countdown: 5...4...3...2...1...and we were off.

I had a plan and needed to stick to it. I would run from aid station to aid station, then take a drink of my water/nutrition mix. It was important to stay on top of the water/nutrition/electrolyte intake if I was going to have any chance of success. A key piece of technology that I had with me was my 4iiii Sportiiii. I had used this little gizmo on Kilimanjaro. On race day, I attached it to my lacrosse helmet, and it would give me an audio heart rate and pace at two-minute intervals. I knew that to achieve the record, I would have to maintain a 5-minute, 30-second per kilometre pace and keep my heart rate below 166 beats per minute (bpm).

Things started off well, and the kilometres ticked by. I got a number of comments from the spectators along the route: "Go hockey player!" "Are you warm in the helmet?" "What the hell are you doing?" "Go Right To Play!" "You can do it, Martin!" My heart rate started off at 105 bpm but by kilometre 15 had hit 161. Along the way, I was joined by two friends, Wayne Benz and Ken Skea, from the Cochrane Red Rock Running Club. I have run many marathons with these guys, and they really helped to keep my spirits up.

My first problem occurred around kilometre 28. The weather was getting hotter and hotter, and my heart rate hit 165. I was also starting to feel some cramping in my legs so I increased my electrolyte intake. I was still on pace, but the heat was beginning to take its toll. By kilometre 34, things were starting to go sideways. My heart rate hit 175 bpm, and I was getting light-headed. Evan, Ken and Wayne were shouting encouragement so I concentrated on shutting out the pain. The next 4 kilometres were a blur. I kept my head up and shoulders back and tried to keep up with the runner in front of me. My head was cooking, and my buddies were pouring water through the vents of my helmet, to help cool me down.

Despite my best efforts, at kilometre 38, everything fell apart. My legs became rubber and started to spasm. My heart rate spiked at 190, and I dropped off a sub-four-hour pace. I jogged the next 3 kilometres in a daze, and I walked the final kilometre. With 300 metres to go, I could hear the cheering crowd in the stadium. I turned into the final

150-metre stretch and was heartened enough by the cheers to start up a shuffle run. I crossed the line and collapsed. Medics were there, and a fellow runner, Ally Johnson, helped me into the medical tent. They stripped off the lacrosse gear, laid me down, wrapped me in a silver blanket and fed me apple juice.

I'm delighted to say that Blaine and his buddies achieved their goals. They not only set a new record but also raised $100,000 for MitoCanada.

My final time was 4 hours, 18 minutes and 58 seconds. Not a Guinness World Record. Would I have liked to have achieved it? Of course, but on that day, it was not to be.

I believe that all you can do is give it a go, and that's what I did. Sometimes one's efforts pay off, and sometimes they don't. As the remaining nine events in Quest #8 awaited and natural events in Alberta unfolded, these thoughts were important to keep in mind.

11

TransRockies and High Rivers

"The three great essentials to achieve anything
worthwhile are, first, hard work; second,
stick-to-itiveness; third, common sense."

— THOMAS A. EDISON

In June 2013 the Alberta floods hit and caused widespread destruction and devastation. One of the consequences was the total revision of TransRockies Quest 888. The plan was to run and bike in ten events, from May to October through the mountains in Alberta, BC and Colorado, a total of 888 race kilometres. Mother Nature would reroute the plans, but I stayed on top of those kilometres.

It was a simple plan. On Tuesday, June 20, I would have my very first mountain-bike lesson. At 2 p.m. I arrived at Canada Olympic

Park (COP) in Calgary and met Rhys Ellis, coach of the WinSport Academy Downhill Mountain Bike Team, which consisted of six athletes whose ages ranged from 14 to 17. They competed at both the provincial and national levels, focusing on the BC Cup Downhill series. The race team was developed from the mountain-bike club program, that was started at COP in 2009. Initially, it consisted of six young mountain bikers who were passionate about the sport. Within four years, the program had grown to 40 riders of varying ages and abilities. Their goal was to follow the Long Term Athlete Development (LTAD) program and instil the "active for life" mentality in young people.

Before we started, Rhys checked over my bike and said that everything looked OK. He had brought along some knee and elbow pads, which I was happy to wear. I want to be clear: I am not good at mountain biking. The week before, I had been out with my friend Tom to Canmore and ridden the Horse Shoe Loop. I took a number of tumbles, leaving blood on the trail.

Rhys wanted to assess my ability so we headed off along a single-track trail. There had been some rain overnight, and I paid the price on a couple of muddy sections strewn with slick tree roots. Before setting out on the second loop, he reduced the air pressure in my tires and gave me five tips:

1. Remember, when climbing, adjust your hips forward on your seat and drop your elbows and wrists.
2. Create a field of view so you can be prepared for coming terrain.
3. Take the path of least resistance; it will usually be the smoothest.
4. In all situations, attempt to have balanced weight on front and rear tires, for optimal traction.

5. Remember to keep your pedals level to stay balanced.

What a difference. No falls and I felt great. I thanked Rhys and headed back to Cochrane looking forward to the weekend and beginning Rundle's Revenge.

Then the rains came.

By Friday, southern Alberta was in a state of emergency. Bridge after bridge collapsed. Highways 1 and 1A were closed. Canmore was completely cut off, and Rundle's Revenge was cancelled. My entry into the world of mountain-bike racing had to wait. I hoped that the third event in Quest #8, scheduled for Sunday, June 30, in Fernie, BC, would still be a go.

Communities from Banff to Calgary and throughout the Bow Valley were devastated by the Bow River flooding. Sue and I pitched in to help victims. On Monday, June 24, we packed food hampers at the Morley Food Bank. Morley is a settlement that is part of the Stoney Nation Reserve, not far from our home in Cochrane. Three bands occupy Stoney Nation territory: Bearspaw, Wesley and Chiniki. At the food bank, coordinator Belinda put Sue and I to work filling Ziploc bags with flour, oats and sugar. Truckloads of food, clothes, bedding and towels were coming in, and volunteers were unloading these and moving them into Morley Community School.

I volunteered again on Thursday. Sam, one of the organizers, met me at the school entrance, and I signed in. I was teamed up with Joel and Daquan. At the time, Joel was in Grade 7 at the school and Daquan was in Grade 5 at Nakoda Elementary School. They were both sleeping in the school, as their homes had been affected by the flood. A truckload of bottled water came in, and the lads worked hard, moving the cargo into one of the classrooms.

I mentioned to coordinator Belinda that the boys had put in a good shift, and she said they were both members of the Morley Cadet Corps, a group of young people who were trying to make a difference in their community. Adversity brings people together. I thought again of Right To Play's motto: Look After Yourself, Look After One Another.

With the cancellation of Rundle's Revenge, I had only completed 5 kilometres of the planned 888 (in May's Skirt Chaser). Next was the Fernie Ultra and Enduro. My plan was to complete the 80-kilometre run, solo through the trails around Fernie, then tackle the mountain-bike enduro, which consists of four timed sections down steep mountain trails. But I knew that even getting to Fernie would be a challenge, given the weather. I would normally have taken Highway 22 south, but the road was partially closed. I had to go via Highway 2 south and bypass the devastation.

Fernie Ultra and Enduro

When I arrived at the Fernie Ski Resort, I met Aaron and Jonathan from TransRockies and picked up my race package.

On Saturday morning, before heading to the start, I had my usual breakfast of oatmeal, blueberries, banana, milk and coffee. The race would be an 80-kilometre ultra with six legs, ranging from 10 to 17 kilometres. At 7:50 a.m., Aaron gave final instructions to the 50 soloists and 30 teams that had registered, with a warning: watch out for bears on the trail!

At 8 a.m. the gun went off. Each leg had a cut-off time, and right from the beginning I was under pressure. On the first three legs, my time was under but, on the fourth, which had a 6 p.m. cut-off, I was right on the wire. One of the organizers told me that if I wanted to finish before the 16-hour deadline, I had better pick up the pace.

This got my butt into gear, and I pushed through the fifth leg in good time. I was spurred on by the gunfire I heard up and down the valley. It sounded like the Terminator vs. Dirty Harry out there. I was a bit concerned: dusk was falling and I didn't want to be mistaken for a moose. As it turned out, the gunshots I had heard were coming from a firing range at the end of the trail. Leg 6 was 13 kilometres, and I had two and a half hours to complete it. Night fell; I turned on my head lamp. Time was ticking.

I finally raced across the finish line at 15 hours, 51 minutes and 32 seconds, with just 8.5 minutes to spare. Luckily, we finished at the Fernie Hotel, so the first things that were placed into my hands were a slice of pizza and a glass of Guinness.

When I woke up on Sunday morning, I made the decision to give the enduro a miss. I knew I would badly injure myself, and I thought I would listen to my gut before charging in. I felt good that I'd added 80 kilometres to the TransRockies Quest 888 bank – only 803 kilometres to go.

Interlude: Helping Out in High River

On Tuesday, July 2, southern Alberta communities were still reeling from the flood. I decided to head to High River, 66 kilometres south of Calgary. I was responding to a call for volunteers from that town's Rotary Club. Vice-president of the club chapter, Patrick Webb, had written, "The work is tiring, dirty and so very rewarding."

As I entered the town, I noticed the first signs of damage. The railway tracks had been twisted like pretzels, and sleepers stood up like fence posts. In the silt-covered Co-op parking lot, I spotted a gentleman wearing a Rotary cap. It was Bob, from the High River club, who partnered me up with Alan, from the Rotary Club of Stettler.

Alan and I worked all morning, helping Owen, a town resident, empty the contents of his flooded basement. Owen was a retired businessman whose business records had been stored in cardboard boxes in a basement closet. The paper had soaked up the water like a sponge. Alan and I lugged wads of saturated documents to a skip. The work was hot, wet and filthy. The silt made everything slimy, and the tubs of debris were heavy and awkward. During a water break, Alan and I chatted with Bob, a neighbour of Owen's. Bob and his wife were in their 70s and had a number of medical conditions. They had lost the will to go back into their house, and they didn't know where to turn. They were overwhelmed.

Owen bought us lunch from the recently reopened Subway. As we munched our sandwiches, he explained the designations given to the damaged houses. Those that had been "Yellow Tagged" were in reasonable shape, "Orange Tagged" needed approval on the electrics and other services and "Red Tagged" had to be demolished. Owen pointed out three neighbours whose houses were tagged "Red."

That afternoon, we removed the rest of the paper and started stripping the drywall. At the end of the day, as I walked back to the Co-op parking lot, I passed house after house, street after street, which had been devastated by the flood. On my drive back to Cochrane, I listened as the CBC reported that 6,000 homes in High River each needed a cleaning team of ten people over several days. It was important that these homes were cleaned up as quickly as possible before mould could set in. The people of High River needed help; they needed people who would take the Rotary motto – Service Above Self – to heart.

Even as I was volunteering, I persisted with Quest #8. I wasn't going to let down Right To Play and the kids.

Kananaskis3

Kananaskis3 was the fourth event in the quest. The original plan was to run three events over three days in the Powderface/Little Elbow area of Kananaskis Country, just outside Bragg Creek. However, Bragg Creek had been hit hard; the bridge on Highway 66 had been destroyed and many of the trails had been wiped out.

Aaron and Jonathan scrambled to find alternative locations. They contacted the managers at the Canmore Nordic Centre and were given permission to hold the events there, despite the fact that Canmore had also taken a hammering from the flood.

On the evening of Friday, July 5, Sue drove me to Canmore along a section of Highway 1, part of which had been repaired, and across several road sections that had been cleared of rocks and debris. At 6:20 p.m. Aaron called all the runners to the start and gave us some last-minute instructions. The first was to follow the orange tape. This was important as in the previous week's Fernie Ultra, a number of the runners had got lost. The second, also important, consisted of what to do if you see a bear.

Black bear:
1. If a black bear is advancing and getting closer, stand your ground. Use your bear spray and anything else to hand to

threaten or distract the bear. Do not run or climb a tree. Bears can run faster and climb better than you.

2. If the bear makes contact, fight back with everything you have.

Grizzly:

1. If the grizzly bear makes contact, curl up into a ball on your side, or lie flat on your stomach.
2. If you are carrying a backpack, place it over your head.
3. Try not to panic; remain as quiet as possible until the attack ends.
4. Be sure the bear has left the area before getting up to seek help.

As you can see, the key is not to get your bears mixed up.

The 13-kilometre run went well, despite the rain and sleet. On Saturday I was back for the marathon. There were approximately 100 runners, the weather wasn't too bad and most people managed to complete the 42.2 kilometres. The next day, we took on the half-marathon. The sun shone from beginning to end, and I really enjoyed the run. All three courses were different but all entailed tackling both steep ascents and descents, often on single-track trails.

Over the three days, I ran 76 kilometres, bringing my quest total up to 161 kilometres.

Gran Fondo Highwood Pass

What is a gran fondo? It's a mass-participation cycling event that has enjoyed incredible popularity in Europe for decades. Loosely translated from the Italian, *gran fondo* means "big ride." These events often cover a hundred kilometres or more and are designed for a large number of cyclists, with a variety of skill levels, from the competitive cyclist to the amateur. The rides are judged by the challenges they offer, often combining steep climbs and long distances. While these are not races, top finishers are often recognized.

The original routing of the Gran Fondo Highwood Pass was, you guessed it, over Highwood Pass in Kananaskis Country, Alberta. This is the highest paved road in Canada and offers superb views of the Rockies. However, the Alberta floods caused the closure of Highway 40 and the TransRockies organizers had to find an alternative. They came up with a route from the David Thompson Resort to Rocky Mountain House: a total of 136 kilometres. I was especially looking forward to this event, as a number of Right To Play representatives were going to join me.

We arrived at David Thompson Resort at 8:30 a.m. and lined up at the start for a photo. Joining me were Robert Witchel, then the Canadian national director of Right To Play; Caroline Ouellette, three-time Olympic gold medalist for the women's hockey team; RTP Athlete Ambassador Becca Fahey, a former teammate of Caroline's; and Anastasia Bucsis, Olympic speed skater and RTP Athlete Ambassador.

At 9:30 a.m. Caroline said a few words to the crowd about Right To Play. Aaron asked me if I would start the race, and I had the honour of firing the starter's pistol. The first part of the journey took us along Lake Abraham. The day was crisp and clear, and the morning sun sparkled off the water. The forecast had predicted thunderstorms later in the day, and I could see black clouds gathering in the far distance. Along the way, I chatted with a number of riders who were doing a gran fondo for the first time. They were all enjoying the experience, despite their concerns about lack of training. There were four aid stations, and the volunteers did a fabulous job of supporting the riders and giving encouragement.

I finished the 136 kilometres in 6 hours, 4 minutes and 38 seconds – the ride left me exhausted. Before the event, the longest training ride I had completed was 52 kilometres. I staggered into the Rocky Mountain House Arena and joined the RTP gang, which had arrived ahead of me. The pasta dinner had almost finished as the group talked about their day. Robert was the first in at just over 4 hours, and Anastasia had won the polka-dot jersey for "Queen of the Mountain" for her age group. Caroline had blown a tire, and she had come in with Becca. Everyone had had a great day, and we planned to get together again for the TransRockies Tour of Alberta Challenge on September 8.

By this point in TransRockies Quest 888, I'd completed 297 kilometres, leaving 591 kilometres to cover. More important, I'd raised $12,745.38 of the $25,000 goal.

TransRockies Challenge

Soon it was on to the next event in Quest #8. I had hardly recovered from the previous one! On July 30 Sue took me, my bike and my duffle bag and dropped me off at Calgary International Airport. I wasn't flying anywhere, but I was there to meet up with a group of cyclists. Already waiting were Ken and Shawn (a father and son duo from Edmonton), Ian from Memphis and Edgar from Mexico. Together, we would be joining a group of competitors for the final four stages of a seven-stage event.

The first three stages had taken place on July 27, 28 and 29 in Fernie, BC, and now the venue was switching to Blairmore, Alberta, where we would take on stages 4 and 5 and then shuttle to Kananaskis Country for stages 6 and 7, finishing in Canmore.

Before the event I hadn't done as much mountain biking as I had planned. I just tried to remember the tips Rhys had given me in mid-June and hoped they would get me through.

We reached Blairmore in 3.5 hours and scurried around to get ready for the noon start. I had brought along my knee protectors and decided to put them on. The fourth stage was 32 kilometres, with an elevation gain/loss of 1200 metres. The first 6 kilometres flew by on tarmac roads with a slight decline. We raced through the town of Coleman, and at 10 kilometres, I reached the first checkpoint in plenty of time. But then, it was up, up, up, along a lung-busting gravel road and double track for 4.5 hours to the summit of Ironstone Lookout. The descent was wild, and I took several falls, bouncing over rocks and flying around hairpin corners.

I made the kilometre-19 checkpoint and went for the finish line, arriving in 5 hours, 23 minutes and 4 seconds, well within the cut-off time. However, I didn't feel good. My shins were cut and scratched, and my thumbs were bruised from hanging on for dear life and making all the gear changes. I was contemplating taking the next day off. It all seemed too much.

I staggered over to the campsite and found my tent. Across the field from me, a couple of guys had set up a bike mechanics shop. I had been having trouble all day with shifting gears and thought I'd get them to look at my bike. After a rest, I met Brian and he put my bike up on the rack. I had purchased my Gary Fisher Sugar 4+ in 2002 in Sudbury, Ontario. I hadn't really used it that much, and this had been its first real test. Brian checked the gears and said that the cables were sticking and needed replacing. I told him to go ahead, anything to make the ride easier. For the first time, I looked around the area at the other bikes and observed the competition.

High-end carbon-fibre machines, super light and very expensive. I left the bike with Brian and headed off for a shower and a meal, tucking into a huge plate of lasagne. In the meal tent, I met riders from all over the world, including the Netherlands, England and Norway.

By the time the awards and route briefing for the next day were done, I still wasn't sure whether or not I would be participating.

After a decent night's sleep, I decided to give stage 5 a try. I knew I might not finish the entire route, but at least I would put some kilometres into the Quest #8 bank. It would be the longest section of the TransRockies Challenge: 52 kilometres with 1800 metres of climbing, some of it, according to the route briefing, on a "primitive single track." I wondered what that might look like – and I soon found out. I added soccer shin guards to my full-body protection, picked up my bike from Brian and headed over to the start line where Aaron said a few words about Right To Play. Again, I had the honour of firing the starter's pistol.

The route out was double and single track. We wound our way through the debris of the Frank Slide and had a terrific view of the mountain cut on the other side.

After 23 kilometres I made the first checkpoint, within the cut-off but with not much time to spare. I pushed on toward the next aid station, but trouble lay ahead. The route was flagged with orange-and-black-striped tape. The markings were fairly easy to follow, but you had to watch out for the sharp turns. At one point it went from a gravel road to the "primitive single track" I'd been wondering about. Imagine someone hacking their way through a jungle with a machete. That's a primitive single track. Branches in your face,

186

The Frank Slide

On April 29, 1903, a rock slide buried the eastern part of Frank, Northwest Territories, a mining town, as well as the Canadian Pacific Railway line in that area and a coal mine. Turtle Mountain, above the town, began to fall away at 4:10 a.m. – over 82 million tonnes of limestone slid downslope within 100 seconds. It was one of the largest landslides in Canadian history and remains the deadliest. Between 70 and 90 of the town's people were killed, many of whom were never extricated from the rubble.

Turtle Mountain had always been known as "the mountain that moves" by local Indigenous peoples, and coal-mining operations may have weakened the mountain's already shaky structure. The wet and mild winter and a cold snap on the night of the slide may have also contributed to the factors leading up to the slide.

Within three weeks of the devastation, the railways and mine both reopened. Three years later, the town's population doubled but then dropped after the mine closed in 1917. In the meantime, responding to fears that the mountain would give way again, the section of town closest to the mountain relocated in 1911. Frank now has a population of about 200 people. The site of the slide, pretty much unchanged since 1903, is now a tourist destination – the interpretive centre receives over 100,000 visitors per year – and is a designated provincial historic site.

hardly enough room to get the bike through. It was a baking-hot day, and I was starting to suffer from the heat.

I arrived at the second checkpoint tired and beaten. I had covered 39 kilometres in 6 hours, 39 minutes and 24 seconds, and that was enough for me. A truck took me back to Blairmore and the campsite.

The next day, after breakfast, participants packed up their bags and jumped on a bus ready for a three-hour transfer to Kananaskis

Country. Stage 6 started at a place called Pine Grove Group Camp, approximately 45 minutes west of Calgary. Originally, we were to ride to the finish at Rafter Six Ranch, but the flood meant a reroute to finish at Stoney Nakoda Resort. This change reduced the route from a distance of 48 to 44.5 kilometres.

This shortening of the route was not much comfort to me. The briefing the previous night in Blairmore had included the words "the Nightmare that is Cox Hill" and information about how some sections would be "unrideable," even for the top racers.

We arrived at Pine Grove Group Camp at 10:30 a.m. and waited around until noon. The rain held off, and we cruised along a well-graded gravel forest road. In the first hour, I covered 11 kilometres and felt great. Then a red arrow pointed left to Cox Hill path. For the next 2.5 hours I pushed my bike up 700 metres of elevation gain and only covered 4 kilometres.

Things were pretty desperate as I had to make the first checkpoint by 4:00 p.m. and I only had 30 minutes to go to cover 9 kilometres. I knew it was not going to happen, so I decided to relax and enjoy the ridge path along Lusk Pass. I arrived at the checkpoint one hour late, but I was not alone. Several other riders had also been beaten by the hill.

The latecomers piled into a 12-seater van, and Ryan from Trans-Rockies drove us to Rafter Six Ranch and our campsite. The forecast for the next day was rain, and as I crawled into my cozy sleeping bag, the heavens opened.

August 2, the day of the final stage, dawned cloudy and rainy. It would be a literal dash to the finish, a time trial, with the fastest riders going out first and the slowest last. The good news about the route was that the 37 kilometres had a thousand metres less climbing than the last two stages. Also, a good percentage of it was in the Canmore Nordic Centre, which I knew fairly well.

We bussed over to Dead Man's Flats, and at 10 a.m., the first competitor sped off, and a new racer followed every 20 seconds. To say the first ones out were fast is an understatement. For example, the first day's race took me 5 hours, 22 minutes and 19 seconds. The fastest time for that stage was 1 hour and 45 minutes by Calle Friberg.

It was my turn to set out at 10:45 a.m. The cut-off time for the first checkpoint was 2 p.m., and I already had a late start because I was one of the slower participants. Also, the first 7 kilometres consisted of a winding path up and down the hillside and I struggled to get going.

I pushed myself, and 17 kilometres later I arrived at the checkpoint with an hour to spare. After some refreshments, I set off on a 200-metre climb in the Canmore Nordic Centre. It was great to recognize some of the trails; it gave me confidence. When I reached the second checkpoint, at the 27-kilometre mark, I knew that if I just kept going I would make it to the finish before the cut-off time.

The last 10 kilometres was the most fun I had during the four days. The path was mostly downhill, and there were lots of muddy sections. I blasted through them, mud splattering. The rain started to fall, but it didn't matter. I was flying, and the end was in sight. I pulled into Canmore Main Street at 3:32 p.m., with 28 minutes to spare. Jonathan from TransRockies met me at the finish line and told me I was the last rider to cross the line of the last TransRockies Challenge ever. In 2014 TransRockies would host an alternative event, the SingleTrack 6.

Later that evening, as Sue drove me home, I finally had a chance to think about the past four days and what I'd accomplished. I had managed to ride/push my bike 132 kilometres, which brought my total to 429 kilometres. I was almost halfway to my "888" target. This event had confirmed that mountain biking was a challenge for me. One needs plenty of technical and physical ability to overcome the arduous trails I had encountered. I knew I would need to work on my skills to prepare for the tenth and last TransRockies event: the three-day mountain-bike race in Moab, Utah, coming up in mid-October. I was feeling unsure and anxious about that, but I knew I would most likely need to compete in that event to hit my target of 888 kilometres.

That night I slept well in my own bed, knowing there was still plenty of work to do. The good news was that so far this quest had raised $29,700 for Right To Play toward the target of $50,000. Despite the problems I'd been facing, I knew that RTP programs for kids all over the world were definitely worth pushing a bike for.

TransRockies Run

Ten days later, on August 12, I flew out to Denver, Colorado, ready for event number six: the 192-kilometre, six-day TransRockies Run. I was keen, despite the cuts and bruises I'd sustained in the previous event.

Four hundred runners were registered. Aaron welcomed us with warnings about some of the challenges ahead: searing heat and running on trails at elevations ranging from 2438 and 3658 metres.

The TransRockies Run is a huge logistical challenge because it consists of six races in a row and the entire infrastructure must be moved for every race. This includes the start and finish chute, breakfast tent, medical and massage tent, shower truck with 12 shower stalls, and 300, two-person tents.

Identity and Culture

The strength of a community correlates with its connection to its traditions, which allow it to plan for the future. The same is true of the youth within communities. Hope for the future is galvanized in connections with and honouring of the past. As Ontario's Provincial Advocate for Children and Youth wrote in the *Feathers of Hope Report* from 2013, First Nations youth find that "going back to their roots has helped them find or restore their identities and filled them with a sense of pride about who they are."

The leaders at PLAY know that identity, culture and confidence are intertwined. PLAY programming, therefore, builds on the strengths of Aboriginal youth and their communities, supporting local cultures and identities. All PLAY programs are designed to respect, integrate and honour culture and traditions, and Community Mentors involve Elders and other community members, who provide a link to the cultural past. When youth are connected to their community in inter-generational events, they feel strong and supported.

For example, in 2013 the power of the powwow and drumming was brought to the fore in Northwest Angle 37 First Nation, where PLAY Community Mentor Whitney Nash planned the community's first powwow in years. She included the 15 youth participants in the PLAY After School Program, kids between the ages of 2 and 12. The community of 200 people backed the event with enthusiasm. The kids raised money for the powwow by running a canteen, and Whitney said that, "everyone wanted to help out." In the end, a hundred people from in and out of the community attended the powwow, and the 50 youth who were there danced and learned Ojibwe from Elders. Five children also competed as dancers – one of whom was crowned "Tiny Tot Princess."

Play can certainly lead to great things!

At 8:25 a.m., on August 13, we were all in the start chute and, with two minutes to go, they played ACDC's "Highway to Hell," a song that would come to be something of an anthem over the next six days. Stage 1 was 34 kilometres from Buena Vista to Railroad Bridge. The first day went well, and each day followed a similar routine: breakfast in the main tent, head to the start line, "Highway to Hell" and off. My run times ranged from 4 hours to 7 hours. Then the best part of the day, a shower. After supper we had the day's awards, a preview of the next day's route and a slide show.

One evening I was asked to make a presentation on Quests for Kids and my work with Right To Play. I had a great response from the group and I was thrilled to be able to introduce fellow runners, sisters Kirsten and Karyn Dibblee. They had followed Marathon Quest 250 and had set up a donation page for TransRockies Quest 888 and raised over $1,000.

Highlights of the event included stage 2, crossing Hope Pass at 3658 metres; stage 3, hanging out in Leadville, the start point for the Leadville Trail 100-mile race; stage 4, running a creek for 2 kilometres, arriving in Red Cliff and enjoying fish tacos at Mango's; stage 5, running the meadow trails around the back of Vail ski hill; and stage 6, finishing in Beaver Creek.

As I flew home, I couldn't help feeling pleased at completing the 192 kilometres. I was now 621 kilometres in! However, looking forward, I knew I had to change gears, so to speak.

TransRockies Tour of Alberta

I had a bit of a break before the next event, TransRockies Tour of Alberta, not to be confused with the actual Tour of Alberta, a profes-

sional cycling event. My buddies Kevin and Roy joined me to participate in this one, an opportunity for recreational riders to cycle some
of the same terrain that the professional teams would be covering in
stage 6 of the Tour of Alberta. It was also my seventh event in Trans-
Rockies Quest 888. If I could complete the 130-kilometre course, I
would have 751 in Quest #8's bank.

Our start time was 7 a.m. at Seaman Stadium, Okotoks, six hours
before stage 6 of the Tour of Alberta would leave from the same spot.
There were two distances to choose from, an 80-kilometre and the
130-kilometre loop. With two minutes to go, I heard the familiar
tune, "Highway to Hell," and we were off. As the sun was rising, we
rolled through sleepy Okotoks and onto the country roads. The first
hour we rode in and out of banks of mist, heading west.

Kevin, Roy and I set up a mini-peloton and the kilometres clicked
by. We were then joined by Gerry, another rider, and our gang of four
ate up the mileage.

Back in the stadium, the crowds were gathering for the 1 p.m.
start of the Tour of Alberta's sixth and final stage. A number of the
riders were signing autographs, and I had the pleasure of meeting
Antoine Duchesne, from the Canadian National team.

I was now at 751 kilometres in my quest, and with two events to
go, I needed 137 more to achieve my goal. It was going to be a close
call.

Get Out Alive: The TransRockies Heli-Run

In between the events of that summer and fall of 2013, I had been
watching a lot of Bear Grylls's TV series, *Get Out Alive*. Bear is a
British adventurer, ex-SAS Officer and youngest ever Chief Scout. In

the show, Bear takes ten teams of two people to New Zealand, where they have to endure many physical and mental tests, including being dropped into a freezing lake from a helicopter, crossing a gorge on

Girls and Sports in Sandy Lake First Nation

Community Mentor Steffany Meekis has been the key to encouraging girls' participation in sports in Sandy Lake, Ontario. Over the course of her first year as a Community Mentor, she noticed a shortage of programming that was exclusively for girls. Steffany knew she needed to create spaces where girls could feel comfortable playing sports, so she started a girls-only basketball program, in addition to her regular After School Program.

Twice a week, 17 girls between the ages of 12 and 14 gather to play ball. Steffany received some great, creative training in the sport at two of PLAY's Basketball For Development coaching clinics. As a coach, she has developed her own unique drills for the girls. In addition to improving their on-court talent, the program has nurtured the girls' leadership skills. Through learning about what makes a good team captain, the girls also came to understand a good leader as positive and open to suggestions, unafraid of making decisions.

By 2015 Steffany had further empowered the girls by hosting off-court team-bonding days and implementing PLAY's Female Empowerment Program (called KWE). KWE brings young women, mentors, Elders and health practitioners together to engage in play-based activities, outdoor education and guided group discussions about health, wellness, confidence and community building. Steffany hopes the program will help the young women connect and build trust with one another, and feel empowered for the long term.

The girls are the "sports stars" of Sandy Lake, and with Steffany cheering them on, they are on a winning streak, both on the court and in their own lives.

a rope, traversing a glacier full of crevasses and building a raft and riding it down a raging river. The winning team collects $500,000. I somehow felt that, as I completed Quest #8, I, too, had endured a variety of physical and mental tests.

The TransRockies Heli-Run, for example, was a sort of one-day *Get Out Alive*, Canadian style. Beginning on September 21, it was the eighth event in the quest and would give me 21 more kilometres for the bank. Seventy courageous individuals had signed up, the majority of which in teams of two. My partner Ally Johnson had returned from a trip to the UK just the day before, after having competed in the ITU World Triathlon Championships in London. I have known Ally for a number of years and knew that she was game for this type of adventure. Our team name was Thunderbirds Are Go! We were ready.

Early Saturday morning, the participants started to arrive at Cline River Heliport, just west of David Thompson Resort in the Canadian Rockies. The event required one team member to complete a 21-kilometre run to the Lake of the Falls, an elevation gain of 1189 metres. The other team member would take a helicopter ride up to the lake and wait for his or her partner, and then they would switch places.

I headed up on the 11 a.m. flight with friends Glenda, Richard and Derek Zamzow, the family who were attempting to complete ten events in 2013 and raise $25,000 for Right To Play. In early June they had held a fundraising dinner and raised over $14,000, so they were well on their way to reaching their target. On the way up, Icefield Heli Tours had us go through a step-by-step safety orientation.

The flight up took only six minutes, but it was exhilarating. We were dropped off at the edge of the lake, and the pilot immediately headed back for the next group. Ally hadn't yet arrived, but as it was so cold, we were given the green light to head off on our leg of the race. The first 10 kilometres were brutal. The summer's floods had destroyed large sections of the old paths, and we were scrambling up and down the riverbank. Ally and I passed each other. She looked strong, and I wished her luck.

At the midway point the terrain changed; suddenly we were running in the forest on a path of pine needles, which felt great under my feet. I came in after 3.5 hours and was ready for food. In *Get Out Alive*, the participants have to eat things like deer heart, eel and maggots. We had BBQ chicken, corn on the cob and Caesar salad.

Another 21 kilometres in the Quest #8 bank. Not a lot, but every kilometre counts.

TransRockies Moab Rocks

On October 10 I flew to Salt Lake City and drove to Moab for the Moab Rocks race. I was nervous on the flight but not because of any issues with turbulence or a fear of flying. No, it was because I knew what lay ahead of me. This would be my final event of the quest. To date, I had completed eight, with activities including road running, road biking, trail running and, the one I enjoyed the least, mountain biking.

That's what was making me so nervous.

Moab is four hours' drive from Salt Lake City. I was staying in a condo with Aaron and some of the TransRockies reps. After settling in, someone suggested we head out for a bike ride. Just what I needed.

We headed up to the Slickrock Trail. According to the guide book, this is a kind of Mecca for mountain-bike riders. To me, it just looked like a bunch of rocks. One group headed out, but a rider named Joanne and I hit the "practice" trail. Right away, I could feel a difference between the mountain routes I was used to, where I would slide all over the place, and this sandstone terrain, where my tires were sticking like glue. I found myself tackling inclines I could only dream about when riding in the Rockies.

When Joanne and I met up with the main group, Ryan suggested that he and I swap bikes. His was newer than my "Old Faithful" Gary Fisher. What a difference! We rode for another 20 minutes before Ryan noticed that a bolt was missing from the front gear of my bike, and that three others were loose.

Back at the condo, I reviewed the stages of the coming event and realized I had miscalculated. I thought I had more mileage available to me. Each stage had two sections, cross-country and timed. What I hadn't realized was that the distance for the timed section was included in the cross-country section. I had been adding them separately. A little more pressure to perform.

The next morning, I rode into town, stopping first at the Poison Spider bike shop. I left my bike with Randy, who suggested I visit the Eklecticafe, where I enjoyed a breakfast of eggs, bacon, potatoes, toast and coffee. It hit the spot. Moab has one main street lined with several funky shops, cafés and restaurants. The backdrop is sandstone hills that have a beautiful salmon hue. I wandered around for awhile before going back to Poison Spider, where Randy had given my bike a thorough once-over. He'd tightened the brakes, lubricated the chain, pumped up the suspension and replaced the missing bolt. Total cost: $3.50 for the bolt.

I didn't have to register until 3 p.m. so I had a couple of hours to fill. I decided to check out the route for the start of stage 1. This took me out of town and along the mighty Colorado River. The sandstone cliffs, overlooking the west bank, looked like the walls of a fortress. The road turned to gravel and headed off into the canyons. I decided that that was as far as I wanted to go. I would save the real adventure for the race.

Registration was at the Moab Recreation and Aquatic Center. We each received a great race package containing a bike shirt, beer mug, coffee beans and beer tickets. Later that evening, at the information meeting, we were given descriptions of the trails and medical information. We were told that staying hydrated was critical and there would be water available along the course. By now, the temperature had dropped and the 30-minute ride, back to the condo, in the dark, was a bit nerve-wracking, but nothing compared to what I would face the following day.

Stage 1: Captain Ahab

The race began at 9 a.m. I hoped to cover 37 kilometres and reach the second checkpoint by the end of the day. I was a bit worried heading out, as one of the organizers had warned us in the briefing the night before about Kane Road. There had recently been an accident between a cyclist and a car, and the cyclist had been killed. This was on my mind. I was riding along, the main pack ahead of me, when suddenly, I saw a body, lying in the middle of the road. Several racers reached him before I did, but even from a distance I could see he was in trouble. There was blood on the road, and he was out cold. Fortunately, in our pack of riders was an ER doctor and his friend, a paramedic. They were able to stabilize the injured guy and call an ambulance. We continued on, with a greater sense of caution.

The scenery was spectacular. I blew through the first checkpoint, and it wasn't long before I reached the second. Soon I came to the Jacob's Ladder portion of the trail. In order to climb it, I would need to carry my bike. I'd done this in previous events, but on seeing this landmark, I felt like turning around. It is a vertical rock pile, squeezed between two canyon walls. It took me an hour to climb the 152 metres. By the time I got to the top, I was beat, but the next part of the route, despite being very rugged, was a breeze in comparison. I ventured on. I was thrilled to make the finish in under five hours, only to find that my GPS read 45 kilometres, instead of 48. Apparently, I had missed the timed stage and incurred a one-hour penalty. I don't know how it happened, but I just had to accept the decision. I was mad at myself because I could ill afford to drop any distance.

Stage 2: Porcupine Rim

At the start line, I was surprised to see the rider who'd taken a fall the previous day. His face was badly bruised, but he was in good spirits. My guide book for this portion of the trail said, "The single track is famous for riding that challenges even elite riders. Cocky riders often take soil samples home along with a serving of crow pie." This stage was 53 kilometres, a good portion of it along a ridge with a 305-metre drop on one side. I was not cocky. I did not want to fall off the edge or take home soil samples so I rode where I could and walked where I could not.

I made the cut-offs for the first and second checkpoints, and I felt confident about the timed section that followed, which proved to be tough, with many narrow ledges with steep drop-offs. Organizer

Aaron was at the finish of this section. I felt good when I rode in and told him that I now felt like a real mountain biker. Two minutes later, however, I went head over heels on one of those drop-offs. Luckily, neither I nor the bike were truly damaged, and I completed the 53-kilometre course in under six hours. I was thrilled.

What I was less thrilled about was the thought of having to ride back into town and then on to the condo. After slowly pedalling for about a mile, I had to stop at a light. A voice behind me called out, "Would you like a ride?" Would I ever! It was Tim and Melanie, a couple from Vancouver, in their truck. Melanie was riding in the event, and they kindly drove me back to the condo.

Stage 3: Magnificent 7

This was it, the final stage in the final event to finish off Quest #8. In my mind I only had to ride 18 of the 50 kilometres it covered, which at the time seemed like luxury to me. Unlike the previous two days, the race was uphill right off the bat. The kilometres ticked by and, at 11:02 a.m., I hit the 18-kilometre mark and had reached my goal. I stopped to take a bunch of photos and appreciate the spectacular view. The rest of the day, I spent riding over rocks and cruising the trails.

I hit the final downhill and crossed the finish line at 3:15 p.m., having completed a total of 920 kilometres over the course of the TransRockies events for 2013. That evening at the Bar-M Chuckwagon, a cowboy-style restaurant, I was asked to say a few words about the work of Right To Play. I told the group that it wasn't until my late 40s that I had started to run and tackle these extreme events. It was a bike trip across Africa that had shown me the power of sport to change the lives of disadvantaged children around the world. When I was introduced to Right To Play, I felt that I wanted to get involved with the organization. Taking on the TransRockies Quest 888 had been extremely challenging, but it showed that we can all make a difference and give the gift of hope to these children.

Quest #8 was finished. Now I had a bit of a break before the start of Quest #9, in March 2014, when I would exchange the desert for the sea.

Right To Play in Canadian Schools

The Right To Play National Inspirational Speakers Series kicked off on September 30, 2013. Thanks to the generous support of Canada's Department of Foreign Affairs, Trade and Development (DFATD – now Global Affairs Canada), RTP was offering free educational and inspirational presentations in schools, across Canada, throughout the month of October. This series would span 24 days, collaborating with more than 30 school boards, reaching 330 schools and over 100,000 students. Whew. It was like another quest!

The focus of the presentations was twofold. First, they aimed to expose RTP Athlete Ambassadors and their life-changing stories to students, in the hope that they will be inspired to get active, set goals and follow their dreams. Second, the presentations would have RTP representatives share stories of hope from children and youth in Right To Play's international programs.

I've been an honorary Athlete Ambassador since 2011, and I was thrilled to be asked to go to Prince Edward Island to speak at ten schools. I arrived at Charlottetown Airport on October 20 and was met by Matt Appleby, a Right To Play representative who would accompany me for the week. Matt had been on the road since the beginning of October, and this would be his fourth week of presentations. As our guide on the island, we were fortunate to have Basil Favaro, a professor in the Faculty of Education at the University of PEI. I have never met a more passionate educator.

As we visited school after school, Basil would introduce us to teachers he had taught. The schools were mostly in Charlottetown, but we visited a couple of country schools, too. The group size ranged from 50 to 450 and Grades 3 to 9. In each school, we had an hour to present, and Matt had the students up and down, playing games and learning about challenges faced by children in various countries around the world. I spoke about my marathons and Guinness World Records, hoping to inspire them to pursue their goals and engage in an active lifestyle. I also asked them for ideas for my tenth quest. Responses included running the Great Wall of China, swimming around PEI and climbing up Mount Everest then skiing down. My favourite was running a marathon on the moon.

Quest #8: By the Numbers

TransRockies Quest 888 (May – October 2013)
Objective: To run or bike all nine summer events (888 km) hosted by TransRockies Events
Location: Western Canada and U.S.

Status: Completed all nine events for a total of 920 km
Donations: $45,190
Matching funds: $123,096
Total: $168,286
Kids helped: 3,366
Funds application: Benin, West Africa

12

Perilous Pathways

"Home is behind, the world ahead,
And there are many paths to tread,
Through shadows to the edge of night,
Until the stars are all alight."

– J.R.R. TOLKIEN, *The Fellowship of the Ring*

Quests for Kids would take me back home. I was born in Devon, a rural English county known for its rolling countryside and cream teas. I have wonderful memories of Mum and Dad taking me and my five younger brothers and sisters to Bigbury-on-Sea on the south coast to build sandcastles. I would soon be returning to this coast but with a very different objective.

Before undertaking Quest #9, Rotary Coastal Quest 630, I decided to run the Yukon Arctic Marathon, known as the toughest race in the world. It actually consists of three races: the marathon, plus the 100- and 300-mile (161- and 483-km) events. For the latter two, participants pull a pulk (a sled) holding all their gear for overnight camping. Just to keep things interesting, every other year the organizers also throw in a 430-mile (692-km) race. This marathon would be training for my next adventure, the 630-mile (1014-km) trek around the southwest coast of England. I was thrilled that accompanying me on the trip to Whitehorse would be my stepson, Calum. He's always great company and supports me in all my endeavours. He has a great sense humour, and I knew he'd have a typically British take on the whole proceedings.

On January 30, at 10:30 a.m., in freezing conditions, the marathon competitors lined up at the start. I took a spot at the front of the pack for a fast getaway. The route was an out and back, and I made great time to the turnaround point. The aid station had hot water, too, so I filled up my CamelBak and set out again, feeling prepared.

I was ready to head home, but I had a concern. My GPS indicated that I had only covered 19.5 kilometres thus far, which meant I would only run 39 kilometres in total: this a marathon does not make. I talked to Glenn, one of the volunteers, and he confirmed the distance. I asked him if it was OK for me to continue down the trail and make up the extra distance. He said, "Fine," and as I headed off I heard him chuckle and say, "Crazy bugger."

I ran 1.6 kilometres and headed back. Over this short distance, the hose on my hydration pack had frozen, but I wasn't concerned: I would just soak it in the vat of hot water when I returned to the aid station. As I ran up to Glenn, however, he told me they had just dumped the water. I continued for another hour and was getting a bit light-headed. I hadn't seen a route marker for awhile, and there were no signs of any other competitors. I needed water so I cracked open the top of the pack and chugged the contents.

I soon figured out that I was lost. Summoning my Boy Scout tracking knowledge, I looked at the ground: no shoe prints, no pole marking, no sled tracks. Conclusion: wrong way; turn around and head back. Three kilometres later, I found the turnoff and arrived at the finish at 6 p.m. in the dark, 7.5 hours from when I started. I was last in the 39-kilometre race, third in the marathon and first in the 48-kilometre ultra. Not a bad day's work! I headed to the coffee house where I had left Calum several hours earlier, and he looked mighty relieved to see me.

After the ultra, the winter moved along uneventfully and soon it was time for me to head to England.

The South West Coast Path passes through five Areas of Outstanding Natural Beauty, seventeen Heritage Coasts, a National Park, two World Heritage Sites, a UNESCO Geopark and Britain's first UNESCO Biosphere Reserve. There is some fascinating history along the route, both ancient and modern. The path starts in Minehead, Somerset, at the mouth of the English Channel. At the 233-kilometre mark is Tintagel, Cornwall, the "home" of King Arthur and the Knights of the Round Table. At 468 kilometres is Poldhu, Cornwall, the location of the famous Poldhu Wireless Station, which was Guglielmo Marconi's transmitter for the first transatlantic radio message sent on December 12, 1901, to Marconi's temporary receiving station on Signal Hill, St. John's, Newfoundland. At the 890-kilometre mark is West Bay, Dorset, the location for the BBC TV series *Broadchurch*, starring David Tennant. One of the highlights of the TV show is the cliff footage. The path finishes after 1014 kilometres (630 mi) at South Haven Point on the shores of Poole Harbour, Dorset.

I have to admit that this, Quest #9, was the event I was most looking forward to. I was born in Buckfastleigh, Devon, and spent many a Sunday afternoon with my mum, dad and brothers and sisters, building sandcastles at our favourite beach, Bigbury-on-Sea, Devon. We'd always pack a picnic. Dad would build a table out of sand and cover it with a woollen blanket. Out would come the tomatoes, cucumber, pork pies and Branston pickle. Hours were spent swimming in the sea and making sandcastles. The day would end with a sandcastle vs. sea battle. We would help Dad make a huge fort with high walls and a moat around it. Then we would go inside and wait. The waves would lap against the walls, and eventually we'd have to scramble out before the sea consumed the fort. I was looking forward to revisiting that beach during Rotary Coastal Quest 630. I thought, perhaps, I might build a sandcastle or two for old times' sake.

The planning for this quest had been in the works for the past year and was only possible through the efforts of two Rotarians based in Cornwall, England, Stephen Lay and David Laud. Stephen was a friend from my days at the Camborne School of Mines. He was now Rotary 1290 District Governor and had invited me to speak at their district conference in March. David was the person who made all the arrangements for me to stay with different Rotary members, each night, as I ran the coast.

On February 27 Sue and I arrived at the Falmouth Hotel, the venue for the conference. The event brought together 250 Rotarians from the 41 clubs in Cornwall and West Devon. My favourite of the conference sessions was the Youth Speaks event. Children from nine primary schools presented on topics like: Should Parents Attend Parenting Classes? and How Can I Mark the 100 Years Since World War I Started? The winning team of three was from Nancledra School with a topic close to my heart: Give It Your Best Shot. They talked about sport for sport's sake and giving it a go. I decided to use their topic as a motto for Quest #9.

On Sunday Sue and I had our first look at the South West Coast Path. There had been a huge amount of rainfall that winter, and the path between Duporth Bay – where Tim Burton's *Alice in Wonderland* was filmed – and Charlestown Harbour was like a mud luge run.

By Monday, March 3, I was heading to the beginning point of the path, in Minehead, the start of the quest.

Section 1/25: Minehead to Lynmouth

At 8 a.m. on Tuesday, March 4, I said my goodbyes to Calum, sister-in-law Lynne and Sue. Members of the Rotary Club of Minehead were at the start line, cheering, and at 8:30 the whistle blew and I was on my way, beginning my ninth and penultimate quest.

Fortunately, Sue would be able to track my progress throughout this endeavour. Prior to Kilimanjaro Quest 95.2, I had purchased a cool little device called the SPOT. It looks like a pager, and you wear it on your upper arm. Basically, it's a GPS system that shows your location on a website, updating every ten minutes. I had also informed the Coast Guard about my progress and the SPOT tracking, and they would follow me on the website, too. This was reassuring because, with the sometimes perilous conditions along the cliff path, I could certainly lose my footing and end up at the bottom of a cliff, or even in the sea.

My friend Stephen ran with me for a mile, and then I was on my own. The route took me to Porlock Weir and on to Culbone Wood, before my endpoint for the day at Lynmouth. The heavy rains had soaked the trail, and in some places the sea had thrown boulders onto the path, which made things a bit slow going. The terrain was challenging due to the dips and climbs along the cliffside. Somehow, I detoured to Foreland Point Lighthouse, well off the path! My pace was about 5 kilometres an hour, so I was an hour late to arrive at Ro Day's big farmhouse in Lynmouth, 34 kilometres (21 mi) from the start. Ro and her husband John welcomed me and made me feel at home.

Sections 2 and 3/25: Lynmouth to Morte Point and on to Bideford

Wednesday's 42 kilometres (26 mi) were another tough slog up the coast; the climbing was relentless. The day before, en route to Lynmouth, I had indulged in a local delicacy, the Cornish pasty. Today I did the same at Combe Martin. The Pasty Power equation goes thus: the pastry is fat for fuel, the meat is protein for muscle recovery, the veggies are good for you and the gravy is turbo.

I later ran into some directional difficulties but finally arrived at Morte Pointe and spent the night with my hosts, Phil and Julia Powell. That evening, I was invited to make a presentation about *Marathon Quest* at Brauton Caen Rotary Club, which was great. I did my best to get a good night's sleep because the next day's stretch of trail would be the longest in the quest: 51 kilometres (32 mi).

The next day, although the mileage was extensive, the path didn't present the same elevation gain I had experienced over the past two days. The first section, along Woolacombe Sand, afforded views of surfers navigating big, crashing waves. The route took me around Baggy Point and along a precarious cliff, after which the path was flat all the way to Bideford.

Throughout the quest, Rotarians met me on the trail to run, to hand off donations and generally kept me company. Today was no different, with Maureen, who had wished me well at Minehead, joining me to pass along £25 for Right To Play. Later that night, at Bideford's Rotary Club meeting, another presenter named Luke gave me £30, which would give one child a RTP program for one year.

Sections 4 and 5/25: Bideford to Hartland Point and on to Crackington Haven

My Bideford Rotary host Jacquie drove me to the start, where I was joined by four runners and two dogs from the Bideford Running Club. One of the runners, Eric, had completed 20 marathons with an average time of five hours per race. He told me he hoped to maintain that average for a few more years – he was 79.

Friday's route took me along the River Torridge, past Appledore and Westward Hoe. The going was good over gentle hills by the beach. However, on the way to Clovelly (one of England's loveliest villages), thick mud created traction problems as the path plunged down to the sea then back up to the clifftop. I gained some Pasty Power in the village, where I told Cathy and Anna about RTP's PLAY program and gathered a donation for the quest. Progress was slow to Hartland Point, and I arrived at the home of Bernie and Sarah as the sun was going down.

As previously mentioned, Rotarian David Laud was my logistics manager for the quest, organizing all the accommodations along the route and making sure I was collected at the right place at the end of each section. He also put together a technical manual for the entire path, with a description of each day's section. For this day's route, he wrote, "Said to be the toughest part of the SWCP, this section can feel very remote and isolated. A day of hard ascents and descents, along with fantastic scenery."

I started early, making for my target, Bude, about 24 kilometres (15 mi) away. I battled wind the whole way there and didn't arrive until 2:20 p.m., certainly behind time. I phoned my Bude host, Simon, to let him know I wouldn't be at Crackington Point until 6:30 p.m. The evening was drawing in, and, as I trudged the last mile, I could see the lights of Simon's car in the parking lot. I was done. This had been an 11-hour day. Simon drove me back to Bude and dropped me off at the Falcon Hotel, where I went up to my room and crashed onto the bed.

Sunday was a day off, and I spent the morning reflecting on the quest so far. I had broken the 1014-kilometre (630-mi) route up into 25 sections, completed 5 of them and covered 220 kilometres (137 mi). I was on schedule for the distance, but the time I was taking to complete each section was a lot longer than I had anticipated. The main problem was the condition of the path. The winter storms had caused havoc with the coastline. Instead of a run, it was more like a scramble. I had planned to start each morning at 8:30 a.m., but on the second day I changed that to 7:30 a.m. I was considering all that still lay before me. I had given a presentation at the Bideford Rotary Club, which had gone well, but, as I looked at my schedule for the rest of the quest, I wondered if there would be enough hours in the day to get everything done.

Section 6/25: Crackington Haven to Pentire Point

Monday morning, after an excellent sleep, I felt refreshed. The first stop along the section-6 route was Tintagel, home of King Arthur and his knights. I could just imagine them sitting at the fabled round table enjoying a pewter mug of mead and tucking into a lamb shank, which is exactly what I had eaten for dinner the previous evening. There's not much left of the castle, but you can certainly get a feeling for the size of the fortifications.

Two miles after that, I ran up against an expanse of gorse on fire, with the path going right through it. I decided to do a Bear Grylls and wet my buff, covered my nose and mouth and plowed through. A few singed leg hairs later, I was out the other side. I rather felt I deserved my pasty and chips in Port William before I headed on to Port Isaac. I didn't arrive at Pentire Point to meet my host, Barry, until sundown.

Because I was so late coming in, I had to do a Rotary Club presentation in full running gear. I think it added to my authenticity – in any event, the Launceston group presented me with a cheque for £250.

Section 7/25: Pentire Point to Portcothan

Rotarian John Barnes joined me for the entire 27 kilometres (17 mi) of this section. This would be the shortest daily distance, and I was pleased not to be putting in ten-hour days on the trail and coming in as the sun went down. The topography by this point on the path was no longer dramatic ups and downs but rolling cliffs and expansive sandy beaches.

John joined me for my first estuary crossing of the quest. Usually, pathgoers take a ferry across the Camel River at Padstow, but I wanted this to be an all-human powered traverse, so John and I jumped into a dinghy provided by another Rotarian, Guy. I hadn't rowed in 40 years and was a little rusty – it took us 40 minutes to cross and get back onto the path.

The rest of the journey was relaxing, and we arrived at Portcothan at 2:30 p.m., the earliest I had arrived anywhere up to this point. Here, Graham would be my host, and he helped me get to presentations at the local primary school and Wadebridge Rotary Club. It was great to see my Canadian running buddy, Kurt Kowolchuk at the club presentation – he would join me for two weeks on the path.

Sections 8 and 9/25: Portcothan to St. Agnes Head to St. Ives

The next day, Kurt and I set off early. I simply didn't want to arrive late at my destinations anymore. Kurt liked the idea of the now well-established tradition of the "Lunchtime Pasty," and we tucked into two excellent specimens in Newquay, at Warren's, "The Oldest Cornish Pasty Maker in the World." Prior to this experience, I wasn't aware that a real Cornish pasty cannot contain carrots.

We ran through thick fog to St. Agnes Head, almost missing Dave Laud. By the next day, the fog still hadn't lifted. For the first four hours of our run to St. Ives, I could only see 20 feet in front of me, and I followed Kurt's heels all the way to Godrevy Point, at kilometre 20 (mile 12.5), the halfway point in the day's section. After that, it was an hour's walk through 5 kilometres (3 mi) of sand.

I was really starting to feel the 9144 metres of elevation gain and loss that I'd covered over the past nine days. At the end of the section, we arrived in St. Ives and met up with our hosts, Claire and

John. I was in constant pain from my right knee at this point so I decided it was time for remedial action. I spent the evening resting up and icing the joint.

Section 10/25: St. Ives to Sennen Cove

Kurt and I left St. Ives and began to run the most desolate part of the path. We didn't see another person for 24 kilometres (15 mi), which took us six hours, and the going was really challenging: boulders and rocks, streams and bogs. As time ticked on and dusk fell, we knew we weren't going to make our original destination, Porthcurno. We had to make an adjustment and decided stop at Sennen Cove instead.

On the way there, we came upon the remnants of the Cornish mining industry. Geevor Tin Mine, which operated between 1911 and 1990, is now a heritage centre, located between the villages of Pendeen and Trewellend. The mine extends about 400 metres out under the Atlantic Ocean, and, among other buildings at the site, the remains of one of the mine's arsenic-refining works sits atop a cliff.

My knee was stiffening up, the temperature had dropped, and my hands were swollen, so we were happy when we reached a sign that read "Sennen Cove 1 mile." We crested the last sand dune and in the distance saw the Old Success Inn. We walked in the door and ordered two pints of Tribute Ale. We were back at Claire and John's place that evening, and I still had to give a presentation, but I soldiered on, knowing that the next day was a rest day. The completion of the first ten sections had taken a toll. A total of 418 kilometres (260 mi) were in the bag, but we were behind schedule.

These rest days were turning out to be anything but. On Saturday, March 15, for example, I returned to a place I hadn't been in many years, the Camborne School of Mines, where I gave a presentation at their annual dinner. I graduated from the college in 1977 and hadn't returned since. Over 300 students, faculty members, ex-grads and friends were in attendance, and they gave me a wonderful reception. I met one of my old professors, Barry Wills, who had introduced me to SCUBA diving off the Cornish coast.

Kurt and I stayed at the Falmouth Hotel, the location of the dinner, but we didn't get much sleep. The students were partying until 5:30 a.m.

Section 11 and 12/25: Sennen Cove to Praa Sands to Coverack

Another 7:30 a.m. start, and within an hour of running, we reached Lands End. We had made good time on this stretch and decided to push along to Praa Sands, about 47 kilometres (29 mi) from Sennen Cove. That night we stayed with Dave and Mandy Laud, the first of a number visits to their home during the quest.

Despite the good time we had made the previous day, we were still about 8 kilometres (5 mi) behind schedule. At Poldhu Point we saw the Marconi Monument, from where, on December 12, 1901, Guglielmo Marconi's first transatlantic radio message was sent to his temporary receiving station on Signal Hill, St. John's, Newfoundland. I tried to call Sue to let her know where I was, but there was no reception. Good job she had the SPOT!

During this stretch we also experienced Lizard Peninsula, known for its bleak but spectacular beauty. The southern cliffs are covered in various types of flora, including spring squill, kidney vetch, birdsfoot

214

trefoil and thyme. Although we craned our necks out to sea, we did not see the area's native seals, dolphins or basking sharks.

Sections 13 and 14/25: Coverack to St. Antony's Head and on to Charlestown

Dave and Mandy had picked us up in Coverack, driven us to their place for the night and then taken us back to Coverack for 7:30 a.m. the next morning. The first 16 kilometres (10 mi) of the 13th stretch consisted of bog and mud, then a granite quarry, where we lost sight of the path and took a wrong turn. We finally got back on track and made our way to Porthallow, at kilometre 507 (mile 315), the halfway mark of the South West Coast Path. There is a marker on the beach, indicating the halfway point and, as I approached it, I tripped and bashed my left shin on a boulder. I didn't give it a second thought as I had taken a number of tumbles. However, this one would come back to haunt me.

That day we were scheduled to cross three rivers, the first at Gullian, then at Helford and Falmouth. At both of the last two river crossings, the ferries were out of order so Dave kindly drove us around both estuaries. We capped off the day's adventures with a short run to St. Antony's Head.

The next day, we tried again to get back on schedule, beginning at 6:30 a.m. This section of the path veered down into coves and back up onto the cliffs. The damage to my shin, which I had suffered the day before, had gone from a bruise to triggering a repetitive-strain injury. I pushed on during the day, but I had to stop running and just walk out the mileage.

Despite this setback, Kurt and I put in over 12 hours. That

evening, at host Stephen's house, I iced my leg, concerned about the next day.

Sections 15 and 16/25: Charlestown to Looe and on to Plymouth-Jennycliff

As expected, I had to walk the section from Charlestown to Looe. After crossing the Fowey ferry, Kurt and I breakfasted and then hunkered down for a rainy afternoon's trek.

Up until this point, the weather had been excellent. We took shelter for a bit in Polperro, but we bucked up and moved along to Looe, walking the most-travelled section. The howling wind and swirling rain caused the sea to boil; waves smashed against the jagged rocks. Kurt and I were relieved to reach Looe at 4:30 p.m. A total of 15 sections had been completed, covering 639 kilometres (397 mi). We were back on schedule, but at a price. All of our days were now starting at 6:30 a.m., and because of my swollen leg, I was walking. I still had 375 kilometres (233 mi) to go.

The next day was a day off, and I spent some time with my brother, Andrew, who picked me up and took me back to his home, in Liskeard. Our sisters, Sally and Louise, joined us for supper: fish, chips and mushy peas with a bottle of Buckfast Tonic Wine.

On Saturday, March 22, the morning for section 16 was clear and bright, and Kurt and I made good time. The first point of interest was the Monkey Sanctuary, overlooking Looe Bay. Originally established in 1964 by the late Leonard Williams (brother of guitarist, John), this operation is run by a cooperative company and exists to provide a stable environment for a colony of Amazonian woolly monkeys.

Even though I had iced my leg the night before, at around the

23-kilometre (14-mi) mark, it started to play up again. After lunch, as I got up from the table, there was a sharp pain behind my left knee. I walked it off over the next couple of kilometres, but for the rest of the day I had strange pains in my leg and back. It was good to meet Rotarians David and Caroline, who would be our hosts for the night at their home in Jennycliff.

Sections 17 and 18/25: Plymouth-Jennycliff to Bigbury-on-Sea and on to Torcross

Section 17 was all about the destination, Bigbury-on-Sea. Many moons ago, on a Sunday afternoon, Mum and Dad Parnell took the six Parnell kids to Bigbury. The objective was to build "The Fort." We had construction-sized shovels for the endeavour. Dad drew out the fort dimensions on the sand, and we went at it. The centre of the fort was dug out and the sand piled up for the outer wall. A trench was dug in front of the fort to take the incoming sea water away.

After three hours, we were ready and we waited. The first waves filled the water redirection trench and the walls were undamaged. Soon the bigger waves came in, and the fort wall took a pounding. Then a huge wave breached the wall and the inside of the fort started to fill up. It was every person for themselves as we scrambled to leave the flooded construction.

So here I was, after all those years, back at Bigbury. I stood on the beach and like King Canute tried to stop the tides. My Salomon Gortex 3D Ultra trainers did well for the first few waves, but soon it was all over. The sea won again.

The next day, Kurt and I were dropped off on the other side of the

Avon River, and we made good time to Salcombe, 21 kilometres (13 mi) away. We indulged in some crab pasties before enduring the rain between Salcombe and Torcross. This 21-kilometre (13-mi) section is already graded "strenuous," and with the bad weather it became "extreme." We were heading straight into the teeth of a gale, and I could only see a metre in front of me. A couple of times I almost dropped off the edge of a cliff.

Eventually, we made it to Torcross, where Kurt and I dined at the Start Bay Inn, on Slapton Sands. Forty years ago my dad had taken me there, and we had skate and chips. I had the same this time. Back then, Dad told me the story of Operation Tiger, one in a series of large-scale rehearsals for the D-Day invasion of Normandy.

Section 19/25: Torcross to Torquay (Harbour)

The night before Kurt and I embarked on this section was strange. Several times I felt the house shudder; it felt like someone was hitting the foundation with a sledge hammer. At breakfast, our host Robin asked if I had heard the pounding and I said I had. He explained that the sea had stripped away the sand in front of the nearby break-water. This had allowed the waves to smash directly into the base of the concrete wall and cause shock waves strong enough to shake the house. These vibrations had been felt a fair distance into the village.

It was Kurt's last day on the South West Coast Path. He had been terrific company, and I enjoyed his stories of his travels around Bhutan and a half-marathon from Everest Base Camp.

We had some ground to make up, so we started at 6 a.m., in the semi-darkness. The route to Strete, our original destination for the day, was straightforward, and we made good time. At Dartmouth we

218

embarked on another river crossing, using a row boat with a motor, and then we moved on to Brixham. That section was tough, but we made it in good time for a final push to Torquay.

That 13-kilometre (8-mi) stretch has a number of beaches that I visited as a kid. A nine-hole pitch and putt still exists at Broad Sands, and at Paignton is the pier where I spent many a happy hour in the penny arcade.

Section 20/25: Torquay to Budleigh Salterton

Our Torquay host, Peter, dropped me back at the promenade in Torquay. I bade farewell to Kurt, who was taking a train to Exeter to visit friends. The morning was cool but clear, and I had a tricky day ahead of me if I wanted to reach my next destination: Budleigh Salterton. I had spoken to my logistics manager Dave the previous evening about the route I should take around Dawlish.

In February winter storms had caused a massive landslide, wiping out the train line between Teignmouth and Dawlish. This had also closed a large section of the path. A little farther on, the ferry across the River Exe didn't open until April 5. This being March 26, I was over a week early and so I would have to take a train to Exeter and then back to Exmouth. This all sounded very complicated.

The detour around the section of rail damage was a real nuisance, but I didn't lose much time. However, a major problem arose with the trip to Exmouth. Dave had told me that the train would leave from Starcross Station, but the station was closed. Time for Plan B. I started to walk the 19-kilometre (12-mi) detour, but after 30 minutes realized that this was ridiculous. Time for Plan C: call Sue. Sue and her sister Lynne were staying in a hotel in Exmouth for a couple of nights. They picked me up and ferried me around to the Exmouth dock. The hike from the dock to Budleigh Salterton was about 10 kilometres (6 mi), and I got there at 6 p.m.

I collapsed into the car and Sue and Lynne drove me back to Exmouth and the Cavendish Hotel. I was glad the next day was a rest day. Amazingly, these rest days seemed to come at exactly the right time. The previous five sections had been daunting. I was getting through them by walking, but the pain in my left leg was barely tolerable. I had completed a total of 842 kilometres (523 mi). It was great to spend some time with Sue. I knew I had only one more block of five sections to go. The final push.

Sections 21 and 22/25: Budleigh Salterton to Lyme Regis to Ferrybridge

On Friday, March 28, at 6:30 a.m., Sue and Lynne dropped me off on the promenade at Budleigh Salterton. I gave them both a big hug and trudged off into the rain. This was the start my last five days on the path.

My left leg continued to bother me, but Advil, Voltarol and a compress of frozen peas seemed to be warding off the pain. By this point, however, because I'd been compensating for the injury, I started to have problems with my left knee and hamstring. They swelled up, which meant limited movement. I dosed myself on pain relievers and, as I ran through the rain, hoped everything would hold together for just a few more days.

The section to Charmouth was odd. There was a huge cliff failure at kilometre 31 (mile 19), and I was diverted along a bridle path. Things were good for awhile, but then I ended up on the main road to

Exeter. There was not much of a shoulder, and the cars whizzing by were a little too close for comfort. It was a miserable afternoon, with a cold wind and driving rain, so I decided to cut my losses and stop in Lyme Regis instead of Charmouth, 5 kilometres (3 mi) farther on.

The next day I had to cover over 48 kilometres (30 mi), so I hit the road at 6 a.m. To my relief, my left leg felt considerably better. I put it down to either the hot tub or the Advil, Tylenol, Voltarol (ATV) cocktail I'd taken before setting out. The sun was up, and I was on my way to Charmouth. Life was great! Then reality kicked in.

More cliff failures forced me to take a detour that turned out to be a wild goose chase around a muddy field and dark wood. Eventually, I came out 100 metres from where I first went in.

The first stop after that brouhaha was West Bay, the setting for the popular UK TV drama series *Broadchurch*, starring David Tennant, better known to most viewers for his lead role in *Doctor Who*. I then ran along rolling cliffs and down to Chesil Beach. This beach is 29 kilometres (18 mi) long, eight kilometres of which I walked. The final 8 kilometres (5 mi) to Ferrybridge was flat, but the sand was wet, so the going was pretty slow. When I arrived, filthy and exhausted, I did have one thing to celebrate; this had been my best day yet: 51 kilometres (31.7 mi), and 12 hours on the path.

Section 23/25: Ferrybridge to Lulworth Cove

On this day, the wheels came off the bus. I really didn't feel like getting up, and things didn't get much better when I said goodbye to my hosts, Alan and Ann, and headed off with an upset stomach.

The first business of the day was to make my way around the Isle of Portland, a limestone tied island, 6 kilometres (4 mi) long by

2.7 kilometres (1.7 mi) wide, in the English Channel. It forms the southernmost point of the county of Dorset. Chesil Beach joins it to the mainland. I spent three hours going around in a circle back to Ferrybridge. By 10 a.m. I hadn't moved a metre closer to my destination so I was pleased when I headed east toward my next port-of-call, Weymouth. Winter-storm path diversions dominated my morning and early afternoon.

First I came across Durdle Door, a natural limestone arch that extends into the ocean from the beach at Lulworth Cove. According to the guide book, the route to this point is "strenuous"; I concur, but this is an attraction not to be missed. It is part of the Jurassic Coast. Arriving at Lulworth Cove, a popular site of natural beauty, I realized I had climbed my third Everest that day.

Section 24/25: Lulworth Cove to Durlston Head

A major issue arose on this, the penultimate day of the penultimate quest. The plan was to cross an artillery range, but the military was firing, so that wouldn't work. I had to take an 11-kilometre (7-mi) detour, which went along several small and one major road. Luckily, at 7 a.m., things were pretty quiet, and I made good time to Kimmerage.

Unfortunately, as soon as I started back on the path, I spotted a sign on a gate with the dreaded words: "Coast Path Closed Follow Diversion." When I looked at the detour, I realized it would add another 8 kilometres (5 mi) so I made my way back to Kimmerage and stopped at a toll gate to ask for alternative directions. The man in the booth told me that some of his mates had been up on the path, and if you used common sense there would be no problem.

I couldn't face another detour so I took his advice and headed back. The sign said that anyone caught on the closed path would be fined £100, but I felt it was a small price to pay. The path was stunning, even though there were several spots where I had to hop over a fence to get around the collapsed route. Halfway along I was surprised to meet a couple who told me they had talked to the coast warden, and he had said the same thing as the toll man.

Waving goodbye to them, I didn't feel such a criminal. I made my destination, Durlston Castle, by 5:30 p.m. I couldn't believe I only had 16 kilometres (10 mi) to go!

Section 25/25: Durlston Head to South Haven Point

Tuesday, April 1, the final day, had arrived. Only 16 kilometres (10 mi) to do in four hours. It seemed pretty straightforward, but experience has taught me that nothing is guaranteed and obstacles can present themselves when you least expect them. First of all, I had trouble finding the path. The fog was thick, and the sea had disappeared. Second, I think my legs knew the quest was almost over. The left one wouldn't loosen up, and the right knee started to ache.

This is a sensational part of the South West Coast Path, the most easterly point of the Jurassic Coast (a UNESCO World Heritage Site). It was too bad I was walking this portion in a pea souper, otherwise I would have been able to appreciate the Old Harry Rocks: three huge, white-chalk formations at Handfest Point. Walking along the clifftop path, I suddenly came to a half-metre-wide section. I realized there was a 60-metre drop on either side. It was obvious that people had gone across this ledge and continued out onto the rocks. It made my stomach turn just looking at the drop.

I backed away and headed to Studland Bay, only 3 kilometres (2 mi) from the finish. Sue, Lynne and Stephen met me for the last push, and we arrived at South Haven Point at 11:30 a.m.

At the finish line were Marlene and Pip Richards. They had cheered me off at the start in Minehead, and they had sent me encouraging messages all the way along. Their daughter Bev was there as were a number of Rotarians. We all headed off to the Savoy Hotel in Bournemouth and enjoyed cake and champagne. The last few days in England were spent relaxing, visiting Sue's mum, dad and friends in Dorset, and Calum at his home in Wimbledon, London. Then it was off to Heathrow and back to Canada.

Rotary Coastal Quest 630 had been the most personal quest to date. It was a gift to go back to Cornwall and Devon, the place where I was born and spent my first 21 years of my life, and explore the coastline. It had been a huge challenge covering the 630+ miles and climbing the equivalent of over three times the height of Mount Everest, in 25 days.

Quest #9: By the Numbers

Rotary Coastal Quest 630
(March 4 – April 1, 2014)
Objective: Run/amble/walk the South West Coast Path (1014 km/ 630 mi)
Location: South West Coast Path, Minehead to South Haven Point, England
Status: Completed 1014 km in 25 days

Donations: $23,776
Matching funds: $0
Total: $23,776
Kids helped: 476
Funds application: Unrestricted, for use in top-priority situations

However, incredible support from my family, friends and Rotary members had made it possible. During the month of April, I rested my leg. The swelling went down, and I slowly got back to running.

The Junior Leaders

In September 1990 the United Nations ratified the Convention on the Rights of the Child, and 194 countries signed. Some of the rights include the right to privacy, the right to an identity, the right to protection and the right to play.

Since that time, Right To Play's play-based, educational programs have helped more than one million vulnerable and marginalized children in 20 countries each week. A strong component to RTP's programs is the utilization of Junior Leaders, boys and girls aged 8 to 16 who play a key role in executing programs for their peers. To date there are over 11,600 Junior Leaders worldwide.

I first saw these young people in action in 2011, when I visited five schools in Benin, West Africa. As an honorary Athlete Ambassador for Right To Play, I travelled with two other Canadian ambassadors, Caroline Ouellette, four-time hockey gold medalist, and Heather Moyse, two-time bobsleigh gold medalist. At Dogoudo School, Junior Leaders taught us a relay game aimed at promoting team work, and at Vedoko School for the Deaf, we participated in a dodge ball game, learning about protecting ourselves and each other.

In 2014 Right To Play began training Junior Leaders in 150 Canadian schools, and on April 15 and 16, Sue and I attended an event, then called Play Academy, at Elizabeth Barrett School in Cochrane, where a group of prospective Junior Leaders learned how to present and teach Right To Play games to their peers. I was excited to attend this lead-up to Canada's nationwide event on May 8, that saw children in schools across Canada celebrate play, promote children's rights and showcase Junior Leaders.

RTP's Jaye and Colin led Cochrane's Play Academy. They are both teachers and had spent the past three weeks travelling the country conducting Play Academies. At 9 a.m., students started to roll in from five schools in the area, from grades ranging from 3 to 10.

After some introductory activities, the students were put into small groups, mixing grades and schools together. The groups were asked to learn how to lead games such as Hungry Spiders, which demonstrates children's rights to security and safe shelter. Protector Dodgeball was another game in play, and it focuses on how kids can protect themselves and others. The students had to show their game to the larger group, explain the rules and objectives, and demonstrate how it is played, set perimeters, organize the other students and answer questions.

Sue and I monitored and participated in the games, making sure all students were actively involved and defining their roles for the presentations. The change in the students from the start of the academy to the end was incredible. It was amazing to see them grow in confidence. We watched as a child in Grade 3, one of the smallest in the session, started out holding back, but once she was in a group and saw that the others would listen to her, she came into her own. Standing in front of all the students, she explained her group's game and its key objectives, with confidence. Sue and I felt she was definitely one of Right To Play's first Canadian Junior Leaders in the making.

***

In the fall of 2014, I ran the Calgary Marathon. I love this marathon and running it again reminded me of when I first ran it in 2003, because my brother, Peter, challenged me to. I was 47 at the time, and running wasn't part of my life – but when the gloves are thrown down by a younger sibling, you don't say no. At the time I was living in Sudbury, Ontario. Not having a clue about training for any race, let alone a marathon, I joined the Sudbury Rocks Running Club and trained for seven months leading up to the race. The club's president, Vince Perdue, could see I was in need of some guidance and became my running mentor. During the winter of 2002 and spring of 2003, I'd head out every Saturday with Vince and the gang. We'd trudge through the snow-packed streets of Sudbury, and I was given tips on clothing, nutrition and hydration. Over the months Vince introduced me to hill repeats, tempos, intervals and the long slow run.

In July 2003 I found myself at the start line of the Calgary Marathon alongside Peter and my other younger brother, Andrew, who had flown in from England. The gun went off, and I flew through the first 2 kilometres. Then disaster struck: I stepped in a pothole and fell flat on my face. Still, I picked myself up and finished in 3 hours and 50 minutes. In total, I have competed in eight marathons in Calgary.

In 2014 Right To Play was going to be one of the featured charities at the marathon. I was definitely in!

13

Squamish to Screech

"Come along! Hop up here! We'll go for a jolly ride. The open road. The dusty highway. Come, I'll show you the world"
– Mr. Toad in *The Wind in the Willows*
by KENNETH GRAHAME

Canada Quest for Kids was the tenth and final quest, a road trip across Canada. The plan was to visit ten universities and set ten Guinness World Records. Not for the faint of heart.

In mid-June 2014 I travelled to Ontario to visit our daughter Kristina and her husband Paul, and our grandchildren, Autumn and Nathan. It was there that, once again, I experienced the power of play.

Autumn was ten at the time, and one morning, as she rode her bike and I walked to a nearby playground, we chatted about my quests and the trip I had made to Kilimanjaro the previous year. I told her that in five years, when she is 15, I would like to take her to climb the mountain. She was really excited at the prospect and wanted to know what she had to do to get ready. I explained that endurance was important, and we would start at the playground.

Over the next hour she pretended that the climbing set was part of the route up the mountain; leaped off the swing set, jumped over an imaginary, raging river; shinnied up the swing set as if it were a group of trees; and balanced across a teeter-totter, "defying a deadly drop into a canyon below."

In the afternoon, I played with 4-year-old Nathan. We went to the pool, where he enjoyed being thrown up into the air and then dunking under the water and popping up, only to be tossed into the air again. He loved it. That night, there were three sleepy heads in the house, all thanks to a great day of play.

Starting on September 19, Canada Quest for Kids would entail travelling to nine Canadian universities and one school and attempting to set ten Guinness World Records (GWRs) for the largest games ever played. I would be busy travelling from a volleyball game on September 17 at Quest University in Squamish, BC, through eight other events to an ice hockey match at Memorial University in Newfoundland on October 13.

This final quest would wrap up the five-year fundraiser I had started in 2009. I felt pretty lucky because Alex Baum, owner of Cochrane Toyota, was supplying a Tacoma truck with a rooftop tent attachment for my trip, and Greg and Elena Noseworthy, owners of Ink'd Graphics, were wrapping the truck in the Canada Quest for Kids logo. Peter Collins, president of Buff Canada, was donating 2,500 neck warmers to be distributed at the universities to raise awareness about Right To Play.

When September 16 arrived, Sue and I climbed into the "Questmobile," the Tacoma kitted out with Rubbermaid containers holding buffs, books, sports equipment and camping gear. After a reception at Cochrane Toyota, we drove off, aiming to travel as far as Salmon Arm, BC. The sun was shining and we made good time. We planned to have lunch in Golden, where we searched to find a McDonald's.

"McDonald's?" I hear you ask. Well, in August 2014, McDonald's had come on board to support Quest #10. When I told my running buddies about this development, you would have thought I had gone over to the Dark Side. Comments like "You can't eat healthy at McDonald's," and "Didn't you see *Super-Size Me?*" came thick and fast. Still, I like to make my own mind up about things so I printed off the McDonald's menu, complete with nutritional facts. I spent nights poring over the data to see if I could construct a healthy McDonald's meal plan for a month of travelling across Canada.

Sometimes when I do a quest I also embark on a personal quest-within-a-quest. In 2010, for example, during Marathon Quest, one of my sponsors was Mackay's Ice Cream in Cochrane. They produce 50 flavours of ice cream, and I took it upon myself to try every one of them. By December 31, 2010, I had accomplished my mission. People often ask me which flavour was my favourite, and it had to be double chocolate with fudge chunks. I can't say I was really taken with the liquorice.

The McDonald's sponsorship gave me another quest opportunity. I decided to attempt to eat healthily, drive 8000 kilometres and not gain a pound.

On September 15, I weighed myself and was 174.6 lbs.

At the Golden, BC, McDonald's, we met the manager, Andrew. We got chatting and he explained that he had started running two years before, had completed two marathons that year and was hoping to, one day, qualify for the Boston Marathon. He had also taken up ultra running. He knew about Right To Play and was a big fan of Clara Hughes. Did you know that Clara once worked at a McDonald's? Sue and I ate Tuscan salads with grilled chicken and bags of apple slices, and drank Americanos. I felt it was an excellent start to the McDonald's experiment.

GWR One: Quest University's Volleyball Game

The following day, we arrived at Quest University in Squamish. Georgia and Mikkala, the organizers of the Quest University Guinness World Record attempt, invited us to a Right To Play Club meeting, where the students talked about the preparations they had made for the next day's volleyball game. They wanted 300 players to participate, from a student body of 700.

Georgia explained that they had to have more than 294 players to set a new Guinness World Record. The plan was to play from 8 a.m. to 4 p.m., with different groups coming in throughout the day to participate.

I couldn't sleep so at 4:30 a.m. I headed out into a wet and misty Squamish pre-dawn. I hadn't run for a couple of days and all the driving was doing me in. I found a 5-kilometre loop along a lit pathway, did a couple of circuits and headed back for a shower and coffee.

Sue and I got to the recreation centre at 7:30 a.m. and waited and waited. It took some time to sort out the net, and the event didn't get started until 8:45. I was a little concerned, but soon players started to arrive. The organization was like a well-oiled machine. To start with you picked up your number and signed in. Then organizers took a photo of you with your number. You proceeded to a desk in the gym and signed in again. Finally, you were checked off at the bleachers. Three video cameras were running the whole time, and a photographer was continuously snapping pictures.

Other Great Days of Play: Beyond Baseball

From 2014 to 2015 the PLAY program in Canada reached more children than ever before, with 3,847 kids participating in programs. Everyone involved with PLAY knows that "playing is not what happened before or after learning; playing is learning."

One of the programs 13 PLAY Community Mentors championed that year was baseball. These mentors created recreational leagues for children and youth in their communities. For example, Chad Kashkish started a league in Aroland First Nation, where twice a week, kids aged 11 to 17 learned how to throw, field and hit. Chad's goal was to keep kids active throughout the summer. Not only did the kids turn out to his practice, but Chad also saw them practising on their own. By the end of the summer,

Aroland hosted a baseball tournament, bringing together 170 participants from five communities.

Before Aroland's tournament, a partnership of RTP, Jays Care Foundation, Kenora Chiefs Advisory and Ontario's Ministry of Child and Youth Services also hosted a baseball tournament called Beyond Baseball. Almost 150 youth from 13 First Nations came to play, found and cement friendships, and enjoy the fruits of all that baseball practice throughout the summer.

The increase in play, as a result of baseball practice and tournaments, has inspired youth in all these communities to continue being physically active. And the friendships and connections formed will certainly last a lifetime.

Hour after hour ticked by, and the numbers crept up. We had to be out of the centre at 4 p.m., and by 2:30, 270 players had taken part: no problem. However, the well dried up. Georgia and the rest of her team had to knock on the doors in the dorms to get students out of their rooms and onto the court.

Once again, I worried, but Georgia and her team came through. By 4 p.m., 310 players had participated in the largest game of volleyball ever and, pending verification, set a Guinness World Record!

After the Squamish victory, Sue and I hit the road and drove through Whistler, Pemberton and Lillooet, following Highway 99 until we reached Salmon Arm. When Penny and her husband Craig, who run the Salmon River Motel and Resort, heard about what we were doing for Right To Play, they kindly offered to put us up for the night free of charge.

The next day we made good time back to Cochrane, where I prepared for my next event on September 22: Quidditch at the University of Calgary.

GWR Two: University of Calgary's Quidditch Match

In 2005, after J.K. Rowling introduced the world to Quidditch, in her *Harry Potter* series, a nonflying version was created at Middlebury College in Vermont. It has grown into its own separate and distinct sport, with seven published rulebooks. The sport may have its roots in the United States, but it has grown, arriving in Canada through Carleton and McGill universities in 2009. Since then, teams have popped up in Australia and across Europe, including Italy, Spain, Belgium, the Netherlands, the UK and France. It then spread to Mexico, Argentina and Brazil.

Questmobile vs. Batmobile

During Quest #10 I was asked, "Which would be the better vehicle for a cross-Canada road trip, the Questmobile or the new Batmobile?"

This was not an easy question to answer at the time. Few details on the new Batmobile had been provided by Zack Synder, director of *Batman vs. Superman: Dawn of Justice* (2016). So I made some educated guesses, compared a number of key areas and came up with a final assessment.

Inside Comfort and Seating Capacity:

The Questmobile seated five and had nine cup holders. It also had cruise control and lumbar seat adjustment for the back. Batman normally travels on his own, maybe sometimes with Robin, so I assumed it's a two-seater with two cup holders. Batman may not want cruise control, but everyone needs back support.

Social Media and Gizmos:

The Questmobile had Bluetooth and satellite radio. I imagine the Batmobile has the same. The Batmobile also has some other fancy stuff. But one thing the Questmobile had that I doubt the Batmobile has is a 120-volt outlet for making coffee.

Other Features:

The Questmobile had one amazing option: a two-person tent fixed to a frame above the truck box. I do not think the Batmobile has a tent, however this should definitely be a consideration, as I'm sure Batman and Robin would love camping.

Final Assessment:

The Batmobile is super cool and has machine guns and a talking computer, but the Questmobile had its very own sleeping quarters.

I'd read all the Harry Potter books, watched the movies and I was still trying to understand the game when I headed out to the GWR attempt. Here is a brief explanation of the rules from the source of all knowledge, Wikipedia: "Quidditch consists of two teams of seven players each mounted on broomsticks played on a hockey rink–sized pitch. The pitch is rectangular with three hoops of varying heights at either end. The ultimate goal is to have more points than the other team by the time the snitch, a tennis ball inside a long sock hanging from the shorts of an impartial official dressed in yellow, is caught." Players are divided into chasers and seekers. In a nutshell, as a chaser, you have to shoot the quaffle (volleyball) through one of the three hoops set up at each end. There are players who throw bludgers (dodge balls) at you, and if you're hit, you have to drop the quaffle. Also, an official runs around with the golden snitch (tennis ball) in a sock, and a seeker from each team tries to grab the golden snitch and end the game. All players, except for the one with the snitch, have to run around with brooms between their legs.

When I arrived at the Quidditch field at the University of Calgary, I was met by Jessica Charles, the organizer and head of the Right To Play Club. She told me that they had had a number of players drop out, so they would be struggling to beat the 90-participant record. A group of us went for a Quidditch demo given by a member of the university's Quidditch team.

I was a chaser and did my best to shoot the quaffle through the hoops. After one and a half hours, we started to run out of players. We had hit the 70-participant mark but needed 21 more to break the record. My friend Ally and I headed into the Olympic Oval to recruit some players and bumped into Gilmore Junio. Gilmore is one of my sporting heroes. At the 2014 Sochi Olympics, after finishing tenth in the 500-metre speed skating final, he unselfishly gave up his spot in the 1000-metre final to Canadian teammate Denny Morrison, who went on to win the silver medal.

Gilmore said he would love to play Quidditch, and he and a couple of buddies ran around campus and convinced students to give it a go. Three and a half hours after the start, the game ended, and 97 participants had played.

After the Quidditch game I said goodbye to Sue: I would be on the road for three weeks.

GWR Three: University of Alberta's Tunnel Ball Game

The drive from Calgary to Edmonton is 400 kilometres, straight north on Highway 2. I decided to test out the tent on the Quest-mobile at Rainbow Valley campground, located in the North Saskatchewan River valley, backing onto Whitemud Creek. Before setting up, though, I headed to McDonald's for supper.

My McDonald's experiment was going well. I ate the oatmeal in the mornings and had sampled a variety of salads at lunch. Supper was more of a challenge. I tried the double Filet-o-Fish but was disappointed. That night in Edmonton, I ordered the Angus burger with a side Caesar salad, apples and 1 per cent milk. I must admit that I didn't eat the bun.

My first night in the Tepui tent (small on the outside, big on the inside) stored in the back of the Questmobile was interesting. Set-up took 15 minutes, and I had no problem climbing up the step ladder into the living space. There are a number of pockets inside, including one designated for bear spray. I quickly settled into my down sleeping bag and started to doze off before I was awoken by a strange sound. Trees creaking? Bears on the prowl? No, it was the truck and car noise from Whitemud Drive. In the end, I dropped off and had a good night's sleep.

In the morning, I headed out for a run along the trails beside Whitemud Creek. Soon I was heading up the Snow Valley ski hill. The run became a lot harder than I had planned, and after 10 kilometres I was happy to get back to the truck.

The Tunnel Ball Guinness World Record attempt was to take place at the University of Alberta Quad, where I met Anuvir and the rest of his Right To Play Club team. The current record number of participants in a tunnel-ball game was 120, and Anuvir told me they had 135 signed up.

The event was scheduled to start at 3:00 p.m., but at first only 84 people were there. Anuvir waited a half-hour, until 97 participants had checked in, then he started a demo game. We all lined up and a game of tunnel ball began. The ball was passed over the head of one person then between the legs of the next and so on. Onlookers started joining the game and soon we had 127 people, ready to play and break a record.

So far, Quest #10 was three for three.

The germ of an idea for Canada Quest for Kids had started back in the fall of 2013. I had been asked to speak at the Right To Play Annual University Club Summit, held at Geneva Park in Orillia, Ontario. There are 27 universities and colleges that have RTP clubs, and 25 students representing 14 universities were at the summit. At the time, I had been playing around with the idea of travelling across Canada and running a marathon at 25 schools. After spending an afternoon with these incredibly enthusiastic and creative individuals, we came up with a plan: visit ten universities and attempt to set ten Guinness World Records.

Over the next nine months, Right To Play representatives Amanda

Powell, Reba Joy and Julia Myer pulled a plan together. Guinness World Record attempts had to be selected, event dates scheduled for each university and sponsors found. A huge plus was that public relations firm Weber Shandwick had agreed to handle all the PR for the quest.

Driving to Ontario

The day after the tunnel ball success, I packed up the tent and headed out across the prairies on a 12-hour drive to Portage la Prairie, Manitoba. This would be a stop-off point before an appointment I had to keep, on Friday, September 26, in Steinbach. I was meeting up with an old running buddy of mine: Albert Martens. Albert had travelled to Calgary and joined me in one of my 250 marathons. He had lined up a radio interview for me, with Michelle Sawatzky-Koop, who played volleyball for Canada in the 1996 Olympic Games in Atlanta. I explained the goal of Canada Quest for Kids and told her that the first Guinness World Record we had set was in volleyball at Quest University in Squamish.

I also began another mini-quest. My friend Wayne had given me the audiobook of *Game of Thrones*, a 28-disc, 33-hour rendition of one of the most popular book series in history. My trip from Edmonton to Sudbury, Ontario, would take about 33 hours. It seemed like a match made in heaven. Or hell – I didn't know which, yet.

My route took me through Kenora, Dryden, Ignace and Thunder Bay, Ontario. One of the highlights for me was the Terry Fox Memorial in Thunder Bay. I got there at 8 p.m. and walked up to the lighted statue of Terry mounted on a granite base. The monument looks out over the bay, and that night the sky was crystal clear; not a breath of wind rippled the water.

Terry's story had been with me since 1980 when he ran his Marathon of Hope. In 1981 I ran in the first 10-kilometre Terry Fox Run with my friend Gerard in Yellowknife, NT. In 2010, when I was running five marathons a week, I would often think of him and his determination and belief in what he was doing, and that would help me keep going.

The next morning I set out bright and early. The scenery had changed from prairie grasslands to Great Lakes, from fields upon fields of crops to jutting rocks and expanses of trees. I drove through the beginning of the season change, the start of the "colours," in northern Ontario. The trees made up a patchwork of reds, oranges, yellows and golds.

For six hours the highway took me around the north shore of Lake Superior through Terrace Bay, Marathon and on to White River.

On August 14, 1914, a trapper stood on the platform of the station at White River. With him was a little orphaned bear cub. It just so happened that, on that same day, an army veterinarian named Lieutenant Harry Colebourn was also at the station. He bought the little bear for $20 and named her Winnipeg, after his hometown, in Manitoba. Later that year, Harry, now a captain, heard that he was to travel to England and await a posting to France. He knew he couldn't take Winnie, as she was now known, to war with him, despite her now being the troop's mascot. So, after arriving in England, he made arrangements for her to be kept at London Zoo. It was there that Winnie became a firm favourite with the visitors, especially the children – one child, in particular. His name was Christopher Robin, son of author A.A. Milne, and the rest, as they say, is history.

After the war, Harry Colebourn returned to England and, upon seeing how happy Winnie was at the zoo, he left her there to live out her days.

A.A. Milne gave Winnie many wonderful quotes. One of my favourites is: "If ever there is tomorrow when we're not together. There is something you must always remember. You are braver than you believe, stronger than you seem, and smarter than you think. But the most important thing is, even if we're apart…I'll always be with you."

My next stop was Sault St. Marie to see my son Kyle. We hadn't chatted in awhile so it was great to catch up. The last time we had hung out together was in 2010, when he joined me in one of my 250 marathons, along the waterways of the Sault. Later that evening, I arrived at my daughter Kristina's in Sudbury, in time for a wonderful meal of fried potatoes, corn and steak tenderloin wrapped in bacon – no McDonald's for me that night!

During the past four days I had covered 3842 kilometres and listened to 28 discs of *Game of Thrones*. My trip so far in "Throne-speak" goes like this. The journey started in the barren mountain lands of British Columbia and Alberta. The truck worshippers hunted far and wide for Double-Doubles and Timbits. Travelling day and night, I passed the wheat and corn fields of the flatlands. Lowland dwellers have built huge cylindrical structures to the Sun Gods and pray for rain. Eventually, I arrived at the great lakes. Shear faces of rock plunge hundreds of fathoms below the ice-clear liquid, where the terrifying water dragons live.

One of the most incredible things about the *Game of Thrones* audiobook is the narration by Roy Dotrice. Roy does an amazing job on all the voices and, incidentally, holds the Guinness World Record for the most character voices in an audiobook.

GWR Four: Western University's 100-Metre Dash Relay

I bade farewell to my daughter and her family and headed out again, passing through Parry Sound, Barrie, around Toronto and down to London, where the next day I would take part in Western University's 100-metre dash relay, the fourth record attempt. The goal was to have a large number of people run the dash over the course of one hour – the record was then 252 participants. It made me wish we had my friend Sam Effah there. In fact, 300 Sams would do the trick. Sam is the fourth-fastest Canadian ever to run the 100 metre, which he did in 10.06 seconds. Not only is he super fast, but he is also an Athlete Ambassador for Right To Play. Sam was a volunteer at the University of Calgary Quidditch game; too bad he couldn't have been there in London, Ontario.

That evening, I set up camp at Lake Whittaker, a conservation area 15 kilometres southeast of London. I was really enjoying the Tepui rooftop tent and slept in until 8 a.m., then went for a run around Lake Whittaker Conservation Area. I spent almost an hour exploring the network of trails in the forest and around the lake. Near the end of the 7-kilometre session, I caught my foot on a root and went flying. Luckily the ground was sandy and covered with leaves. I certainly didn't want to get injured with what I had coming up that afternoon.

Emma, organizer of Western's Right To Play Club, had suggested that I park at the TD Stadium, where the record attempt was going to take place. The current record was 252 people, and to beat that, each person would have to average 14 seconds for the distance. A very tall order.

We had 160 on the field and then word went out to all the sports teams at Western. Over the next hour, the track, rugby, soccer and football teams all turned up. With ten minutes to go, we had 214 ready to run, so students went into the gym and dragged people off the treadmills to participate. At 5:15 p.m., the gun went off. Round and round the runners went, handing over the baton every 100 metres. At the 59-minute mark, 252 runners had completed their dash and the record had been equalled. In the last 60 seconds, four more runners ran their sections and as the last runner (#256) crossed the finish line, on the hour mark, a huge cheer went up.

These Guinness World Record events were beginning to shred my nerves!

That night I listened to the crickets chirruping and slept well until about 4:30 a.m., when the heavens opened and the tent got its christening. The rain lashed down, but the tent stayed dry; being six feet off the ground certainly helped. I would like to say it was a rhythmic sound, but it was more like the hammering of a drum.

GWR Five: Wilfrid Laurier's European Handball Game

The next day's drive was a short one, 114 kilometres to Waterloo. Colin from Wilfrid Laurier University's Right To Play Club had booked a site for me at Laurel Creek Conservation Area. He met me at the gate with two other RTP Club members, and they showed me around the park. We chatted about the next day's European handball Guinness World Record attempt, and he let slip that RTP's founder and CEO Johann Koss would be coming. In 2010 Johann had joined me on one of my 250 marathons, and I was thrilled that he would be participating in the tenth and final quest.

At 9:30 a.m. on Wednesday, October 1, I met Jocelyn and other members from the RTP Club at University Stadium. She told me that over 100 people had signed up on Facebook.

At 10:45 a.m. Johann Koss arrived with Reba and Kyla from Right To Play's head office. At 11:30 the whistle blew, and the attempt to set a Guinness World Record for the most people to play in a game of European handball began. The only problem was that we started with 54 people and needed another 46 to achieve our goal. Over the next two hours, people trickled in. RTP representatives made calls and sent out tweets. They found a soccer team and pulled people in off the street. By 1:20 p.m. the game was finished, and a total of 105 had played. Another nail-biter!

Staying in the tent night after night had been fun, but I was happy to swap it for a comfy bed at my friends David and Krista's place, in Toronto. The next day, Thursday, October 2, was the midpoint for the quest. At midpoint in a game, a team reflects on the first half, considers lessons learn and looks forward to the second half. True to tradition, that afternoon I met with members of the Right To Play team, Shannon, Reba, Kyla and Julie, and we reflected on events thus far.

Five Guinness Records had been attempted and, pending verification, achieved. One thing we had certainly learned so far was only to expect half the number signed up on Facebook to actually arrive. So far, Quest #10 had raised $46,106, and I'd travelled 6540 kilometres in the Questmobile, which had performed perfectly. I'd also eaten 19 McDonald's meals and finished *Game of Thrones* Audiobook 1.

GWR Six: Dublin Heights Elementary and Middle School's Ball Hockey Game

It was time to tackle the sixth Guinness World Record attempt, ball hockey at Dublin Heights Elementary and Middle School. This event had been organized by a joint effort of the RTP clubs at University of Toronto, Ryerson University and Humber College, and they had decided to involve a school, which would eliminate the concern about getting enough participants. Before the game began, I gave a presentation to the students of the school with Right To Play representative Nancy.

The Grade 1 to 8 students from Dublin Heights were assembled in the gym when Nancy gave an overview of the charity and what they do. I then came up and told the students about my bike trip across Africa, running 250 marathons in one year and climbing Mount Kilimanjaro in 21 hours. I then explained my tenth quest, visiting ten universities to attempt ten Guinness World Records in 26 days.

At the end of the talk I gave a copy of *Marathon Quest* to the principal, Dan. As I was returning to my seat, I was stopped by a student in a wheelchair, a small boy with the biggest smile I'd seen in a long time, who said, "Can I have a book?" I dug out a copy, signed it and gave it to him. He told me his name was Daniel and that he was in Grade 8. I asked him about the casts he had on both legs, and he told me that he had broken one swimming and the other playing basketball.

We said goodbye and headed outside for the ball hockey world record. All afternoon, as students went on and came off the playing field, Daniel would wave his short plastic hockey stick and shout encouragement to the players. I asked Daniel's mother if he was going to play, but she told me he was unable to because he had brittle bone disease. Later in the afternoon it clouded up and began to rain, but Daniel didn't move. He continued cheering on the players. At the end of the game – we had 103 participants in all, enough to beat the 60-player record – we went into the school. I met Daniel and his mother, who was drying his hair. It had gone all spiky and he was laughing his head off.

Sometimes you meet people with a life force that burns like a Roman candle. Daniel improves the lives of everyone he meets. You can't feel down when you're around him. In fact, our brief meeting gave me extra resolve to carry on and finish my quests. He'd given me the strength to finish the job.

GWR Seven: McGill's Love Clap

On Sunday, October 5, I said goodbye to David and Krista after three wonderful nights of sleeping in a real bed and left Toronto for Montreal to meet a group of McGill students at a McDonald's, in the city. I had been doing this off and on throughout the trip, taking part in the "10,000 coffees initiative," wherein experts talk to leaders of the future about their experiences in work and life. The group I met in Montreal was the one organizing the seventh Guinness World Record. They would be attempting to have the most people play Love Clap, a fun pat-a-cake game for kids, and they thought the record they had to beat was 300. Unfortunately, the week before I met with them, the group had received some bad news, when they were told by Guinness that the current record now stood at 645 people. They were desperately scrambling to get more participants.

They contacted Dr. Phil Gold, a pioneer cancer researcher and professor at McGill, and he agreed that his class could participate at the beginning of the lecture, at 9:30 a.m. This was great, but that would be only 545 students. Still more were needed.

At 9 a.m. some club members and I headed over to FACE (Fine Arts Core Education) High School just across the road from the university. One of the club members with us, Jasmine, had studied there for a couple of years and said that one of the teachers would help us. The teacher was terrific and told me to make a pitch to the class. She said that whoever wanted to go could. At 9:10 a.m. we all headed out – it was rather like the Pied Piper of Hamlin leading a group of 40 kids over to an auditorium.

By 9:30 a.m. the lecture theatre was packed. Andrew from the club demonstrated how to play Love Clap, and then we all joined in. Fourteen seconds later, it was over, and a huge cheer went up. Did we beat the current GWR? Nobody was sure. I had to hit the road as I was heading to New Brunswick, nine hours away. I was at my friends Tom and Ulrica's place in Fredericton, when, at 9 p.m., Andrew and the whole RTP Club called. There had been 671 participants – they had done it. I couldn't help thinking, "That's seven for seven!" And the next day, I hoped we would make it eight for eight at the University of New Brunswick, playing their game of Capture the Flag.

GWR Eight: University of New Brunswick's Capture the Flag Game

I had an excellent night's sleep. It was great to see Tom again. He was the fellow, way back in 2009, who introduced me to Right To Play. During that year we set up Kids-U-Can and raised $10,000 for the organization. This had inspired me and, consequently, later that year, I decided to attempt to run 250 marathons in one year and raise money for Right To Play.

That morning, however, I only wanted to run 10 kilometres. I headed out the door and tried to find a trail that Tom had told me about. I had no luck and ended up running some back roads along a bed of orange, yellow and red leaves. These runs certainly helped clear my mind and relieved some of the stress. Every attempt, apart from the ball hockey, had been a scramble to get enough participants. I also knew that verification for these records would be won or lost in the documentation sent to Guinness.

Registration was scheduled for 5:45 p.m., and the game was to begin at 6:30. Tom and I got there at 5 p.m. and hung up banners and posters. We met up with organizers Shea and Aly, and slowly the players trickled in. However, by 6:30 we only had 160 participants – we needed at least 251. This was getting exasperating. Time for action. Volunteers were sent to find more players on campus. The floodlights came on and dusk was falling. Several people left because they couldn't wait any longer. Things were looking desperate.

By the time the game started at 7:35, we had 260 players, and everyone heaved a sigh of relief. That night, as Tom and I drove back to his house, I thought, "Only two more to go, Ultimate Frisbee at Mount Allison in Sackville, New Brunswick, and ice hockey at Memorial University in St. John's, Newfoundland."

GWR Nine: Mount Allison's Ultimate Frisbee Game

The next day, I looked at the map and figured the road trip was half done. I said goodbye to Tom and Ulrica and continued on my way to Sackville, travelling 220 kilometres, the route awash in fall colours. I had a meeting with the Mount Allison Right To Play Club members, and I didn't want to be late.

When I arrived, I was met by Alex, one of the main organizers of the Ultimate Frisbee Guinness World Record attempt. By 8 p.m. we were joined by 12 members of her committee, and we chatted about the next day's event. They were all very nervous about having enough people to make it a go. I assured them that they weren't the first group to have that feeling.

I had never played Ultimate Frisbee before, so I did a bit of research. Wikipedia told me that "Ultimate is a limited-contact field team sport played with a flying disc (Frisbee). Points are scored by passing the disc to a teammate in the opposing end zone. Other basic rules are that players must not take steps while holding the disc (maintain a pivot), and interceptions and incomplete passes are turn-overs [giving it to the other side]."

What really intrigued me about the game is that it apparently began during the U.S.'s rebellious 1960s and has never employed referees to enforce the rules – instead, all players are relied upon to play a fair game, calling their own fouls. In some competitions now, however, observers are used to help in disputes, and it looks like the new professional leagues are empowering referees, but I liked the idea of a game so invested in fair play.

At 4:30 p.m. I headed down to the soccer field on the Mount Allison campus and met up with the Right To Play volunteers. By 6:10 they had the required 83 participants and the game began. Each side had seven players, and they would switch out after ten minutes or when a point was scored, whichever happened first.

I was on the third shift and had a blast running around in the mud trying to catch the flying disc. At the end of a particular play, I made a long run upfield and caught the saucer in the end zone, making my first-ever point. We finished the game by 8 p.m., with a total of 121 players involved and a new record set.

The next day, I had to drive east to North Sydney, Nova Scotia, and then catch the overnight ferry across to Newfoundland.

GWR Ten: Memorial University's Ice Hockey Game

Before heading out to Memorial University, I went for a run in Sackville's Waterfowl Park. It's an incredible place with wooden boardwalks winding their way through the rushes and across marshlands. The day was bright and cool, and I took some beautiful photos of the sun reflecting off the water.

Then I hopped in the Questmobile to experience more amazing scenery: from rolling countryside to ocean views. When I saw a sign for the golden arches with the slogan "Port Hawkesbury: McLobster," I knew I was in the right place. I reflected that my McDiet was going well. I would be checking my weight after the ice hockey game, and I hoped I would have successfully eaten my way through Canada's McDonald's restaurants without having gained a pound.

Upon arriving in Newfoundland, my first port of call was Corner Brook, two hours up the coast from the ferry dock. I had time to spare so I headed into Gros Morne National Park. The road took me up and down the rugged terrain, and the ocean cut into the craggy coastline, affording spectacular views.

After lunch I gave Jared from Memorial University a call. I asked him how it was going, and he said, "Not good." He was experiencing the same difficulty as so many other GWR organizers had, struggling to get enough players out for the hockey event. He told me he was going to hit a bunch of arenas that day and put up posters. I told him that I would do a big push on social media that night and see if we could turn the tide for the 9 a.m. start on October 13. The scenery on the drive to St. John's was stunning and harsh: barren rock, stunted trees and water everywhere.

When I arrived at my final destination on Canada Quest for Kids, St. John's, Newfoundland, I'd driven over 10,000 kilometres for this game, my trusty hockey gear in the back of the Questmobile.

I made it to the city by 5 p.m., and just as I settled into the B & B, Jared called. He wanted to come over, pick me up and head out to the arena where the game would take place the next day. Once there, we talked to moms and dads about having their kids play in the GWR game, and they were keen.

After our recruitment session, Jared took me to an Irish pub on George Street for clam chowder, a pint of Yellow Belly Amber and some traditional Newfoundland music. I had to cut my time there short, though, because I had to collect Sue from the airport. It was great to see her after all my days on the road.

The next day after breakfast, we headed out to the arena. Jared was there with his dad, Mike, Myfanwy, co-organizer of the event, and a group of Right To Play volunteers. At 9 a.m. the first players started to arrive and the record-breaking attempt got under way.

I was on the first line with Peter Soucy, AKA Snook. Peter is a Newfoundland comedian, actor and radio host. We played ten minutes, then the next group, a team from a junior hockey association in St. John's, came onto the ice.

Unfortunately, by midday we were running low on players, and everyone was on Twitter and Facebook, trying to recruit more participants. The players who were there put in long shifts, keeping the game going in hopes of a surge of new players. But after six hours of play, we were down to three on three plus the goalies. The last player to join us was 8-year-old Jack, who was thrilled to get on the ice. We played for 30 minutes more, and Jack scored ten goals.

Jared called the game at 4:30 p.m., and the attempt was over. He and Myfanwy were disappointed but keen to build on what they had accomplished – even though they were unable to recruit enough players for a GWR, they had created awareness of Right To Play in St. John's and were keen to use that as a springboard in the near future. As I told them, in life you have to "give it a go," and they certainly did that.

There was a price to pay for the four, 20-minute shifts I played in St. John's. Everything ached, and at the B & B, it was a struggle just getting down the stairs for breakfast.

Quest #10: By the Numbers

Canada Quest for Kids
(September 19 – October 14, 2014)
Objective: Complete ten Guinness World Records at ten universities across Canada
Location: Canada
Status: Completed nine

Guinness World Record's attempts, one verified
Donations: $65,029
Matching funds: $0
Total: $65,029
Kids helped: 1,301
Funds application: Unrestricted

Before leaving the city, Sue and I visited the Terry Fox statue at the end of Water Street. The small garden there is known as the Terry Fox Mile Zero Memorial Site, where, on April 20, 1980, Terry dipped his toe into the Atlantic Ocean before starting his Marathon of Hope. The statue is slightly larger than life. Terry's words, etched in stone, still ring true today: "I just wish people would realize that anything's possible if you try; dreams are possible if you try."

The McQuest Is Over

My goal to drive across Canada, eating at McDonald's all the way and not gaining a pound was a success. On September 17 I weighed in at 174.6 pounds, and on October 14, 10,000 kilometres and 31 McDonald's meals later, I weighed in at 171.6 pounds. I'd actually lost three pounds.

But, as they say, the devil is in the details. In total I ate 31 meals with 79 food/drink items, at 25 different locations in 8 provinces over 27 days. These items were: 1 McLobster (no bun), 1 Filet-o-Fish, 2 bottles of water, 3 cups of tea, 3 Egg McMuffins, 4 apples, 4 cookies, 4 Angus burgers (no buns), 5 McWraps, 7 salads (large and side), 9 bowls of oatmeal, 17 coffees (Americano and Mocha), and 19 cartons of milk.

Of course, one should consider that different weigh scales were used for the weigh in and weigh off, and other meals were taken at other food establishments and homes. I ran 85 kilometres and participated in ten GWR events.

Overall McDonald's provided good food options and excellent service. A couple of suggestions include: get rid of the Filet-o-Fish, it looks like and tastes like a breaded beer mat. Why not introduce

McSalmon in Canada, like they have in Norway? Also, a soup would be good, say a McMushroom. Looking to the future, maybe a McPub with beer from a McMicrobrewery. McCheers!

***

I was 11 when my mum and dad took over an old, sprawling property from my grandmother. In the grounds was a tennis court, however, tennis hadn't been played on it for a number of years. It was overgrown and looked like a cow patch. One spring and summer, Dad cut down the brambles, rolled the grass and built a wooden fence with netting all around the court.

My job was to line the tennis court. I found the dimensions in an old *Encyclopedia Britannica* and, using a huge ball of string, staked it out. Next, I painted the string with creosote, killing the grass. Finally, I mixed up a bucket of lime and water, carefully brushing it along the burned strip and, voila, a tennis court was born. My family, friends and I played many hours of tennis together on that court. But as with all good things, life gets in the way and at the time of Quest #10, I hadn't played in years. I had somehow wanted to include tennis in the quests – but it didn't work out.

However, while I was in Fredericton, I met Rufus Nel through my friend Tom. Rufus is a triathlete, an ultra runner and the head professional at the Abony Family Tennis Centre. After an hour of chatting, an idea was born: 24 hours of tennis in support of Right To Play. So, on December 4, at 6 p.m., I got ready to step on to the court for the first time in years. Tom had joined Rufus and me in creating this event, and he had lined up an amazing schedule. For the first 45 minutes, I played New Brunswick Premier Brian Gallant. It was a hard-fought affair and my elbow was sore. Not a good thing with 23 hours to go.

As Wednesday evening turned into night, players arrived to take their turns. I had all my supplies at hand: sandwiches, brownies, bananas and coffee. After six hours, fatigue set in. My elbow was tender and my legs were starting to feel heavy. By the time participant Sherri arrived, I needed another coffee. Sherri was a natural, and she played on, even when the lights went out at the centre (fortunately, some emergency lighting kicked in). It wasn't perfect, but we were able to continue to rally in the semi-darkness, the ghostly ball travelling backward and forward over the net.

Night turned to day, and groups of children started to pour in from Park Street, George Street, Fredericton High, Chief Harold Sappier, Devon Middle and Montgomery schools. Balls were flying everywhere, and the kids were having a blast. The hours and minutes ticked by, and finally it was 5:55 p.m., only five minutes to go. Tom and Rufus joined me for the final game, and as the clock struck 6 p.m., a huge cheer went up: 24 hours of tennis were in the bag.

The tennis marathon was a tremendous success and raised over $4,000 for Right To Play. Amazingly, 350 children had played, and I had relived some wonderful memories of playing as a kid with Mum and Dad.

As I prepared for my final event of 2014, the fifth Marathon Quest 250 Walk/Run, the news about the GWRs was not good. The universities had been struggling with the documentation needed by Guinness. I remember Mike Empric, the GWR adjudicator who had approved the longest game of soccer record, telling me that only 5 per cent of the records applied for actually are set, due to insufficient documentation. The requirements are extremely rigorous, and issues arose in all the attempts except ball hockey. Officially, only one of the nine records was achieved. This was a huge disappointment to many individuals involved, but it didn't dampen their sense of accomplishment. A total of $65,000 had been donated to Right To Play, and awareness of the organization had significantly increased across the country as a result of the record attempts. However, the biggest win was that 1,300 more children had been given the gift of hope.

Quests for Kids was done, and on December 31, 2014, I had mixed emotions as I headed down to the Spray Lake Sawmills Family Sports Centre for the Marathon Quest 250 Run/Walk. Long-time supporters Angie, Hiro and Lourdes signed up promptly at 8 a.m., and by the time 9 a.m. rolled around, there were 25 runners ready to go. I did the countdown from ten, blew my trusty whistle and away we went.

Throughout the day, runners and walkers came out to do their thing. Blanche Ellis, 82, did her first 2-kilometre. Her son Roy gave her a hand because of the footing, but she was thrilled as she crossed the line. Moms and dads supported their kids, and every child received a medal sponsored by the Calgary Marathon. We were lucky with the weather. In previous years we had run in –20 and –30°C, but that day it was –6°C, with a light wind.

My run went well until the 32-kilometre mark. I hadn't done a very good job of hydration or nutrition, and I was feeling a bit lightheaded. I was running with my friend Ally, and she was feeling the same. As we were moaning and groaning, we met Gulled along the path. Gulled is from Somalia and was doing his first half-marathon. He told us that as a child he had half a day a week free from work, but even during that time, he was not allowed to play. He totally believes in what Right To Play is doing and that it is a crime that children do not have the right to play in many areas of the world.

After speaking with Gulled, Ally and I were re-energized. Many runners joined in for the final push. Sue grabbed my hand for the last 100 metres, and we reached the finish line together.

With the help of thousands of people from around the world, we had eclipsed our $1 million target and raised over $1.3 million for Right To Play, which would provide programs for over 27,000 children. It had been an amazing five years, but I was tired, and, as I drifted off to sleep, I wondered what the future would bring. Little did I know that in a few short months my world would be turned upside down.

Quests for Kids: By the Numbers

Quests for Kids (January 1, 2010 – December 31, 2014)
Objectives: Ten quests in five years, raise $1m for RTP and help 20,000 kids
Locations: Canada, Cook Islands, Tanzania, USA and England
Status: Completed ten quests in five years

Donations: $669,922
Matching funds: $697,077
Total: $1,366,999
Kids helped: 27,340
Funds application: Benin, West Africa, and the rest of the RTP world

14

The Clot

"Most of our obstacles would melt away if,
instead of cowering before them, we should make
up our minds to walk boldly through them."

— ORISON SWETT MARDEN, author

*Sue and I decided to take a holiday in Cuba. Quests for Kids was
over, and when I returned from our trip, I began to focus on my
speaking career. The road ahead looked clear, until a pretty big
roadblock emerged, surprising both of us.*

At the beginning of 2015, in order to celebrate finishing Quests
for Kids, Sue and I took a fantastic trip to Cuba. We visited Havana,
talked to locals about the changing politics in the country, learned
about the culture and history of the nation, enjoyed the beauty of
the island and its people and mused about the future. As I ran along

some of Cuba's coastal pathways, I was reminded of the South West Coast Path and my struggles there in March 2014.

When we arrived back in Cochrane, I was ready to give 100 per cent to my new career as a professional speaker. Over the last couple of years, I had already given many presentations, some paid and others not. I wanted to see if I could a make a go of this venture and had joined the Canadian Association of Professional Speakers.

In early February 2015, we hosted a family from Australia. I had heard about them from a friend of mine, Andy Lopata. Paul and Jacqui Brown, with their son Ben, wanted to get people off the couch, so they had embarked on a journey to participate in 50 sports in 50 weeks. During the time they stayed with us, I introduced them to snowshoeing, lacrosse and curling. On February 12 we were at the Cochrane Curling Club, and I started to get a migraine. I don't often get headaches, and the last time I'd had a migraine was 30 years before. Over the next couple of days, my headaches became worse and worse, and my family doctor, Bill Hanlon, gave me some powerful painkillers. He also booked me in for a CT scan.

On February 20 I did a presentation, Play: A Global Perspective. My head was splitting and I was happy to wrap it up and get home. Things didn't get any better over the weekend, so on Tuesday I had my eyes checked, but that test didn't set off any alarm bells.

A couple of days later, I was booked to give a keynote speech at the Recreation Connections Manitoba Conference, in Winnipeg. I flew out to Manitoba but was still in pain when I arrived. I spoke with Susanne, the conference organizer, about the situation. I had planned to spend a day preparing for my presentation but ended up trying to sleep the headache away. By evening, I was getting worse, so I told Susanne I needed to get to the Emergency Room. Her colleague, Cory, took me to Grace Hospital, where I was given a CT scan. I then returned to the hotel to endure a terrible night. Also, I couldn't keep anything down and, by morning, I had to tell Susanne that I wouldn't be able to do my presentation. Fortunately, she had a replacement standing by. I went back to bed.

Mid-morning, I got a call. The hospital wanted to admit me immediately. The scan had revealed an extensive blood clot within my brain. Cory drove me and, within an hour, I was hooked up to an IV and getting morphine shots every 15 minutes. The next day, I was transferred to the Health Sciences Centre. What followed was a blur of doctors, nurses and specialists checking me all hours of the day and night. Then Sue arrived and found I had been put into an induced coma.

I was an absolute mess. After CT scans and an MRI, I was found to have a cerebral venous sinus thrombosis, a clot in my brain travelling along a vein in my sinus cavity. I was on morphine and had to have spinal fluid, which had built up between my brain and skull, drained to relieve pressure. The clot was pressing on my optic nerve, and my left eye had turned in, affecting my vision and coordination.

In the past I had chosen to take on many challenges, but this challenge had chosen me. I had no control over the situation. I didn't know what I was facing and whether or not I had – as in all the various challenges I had taken on in my Quests for Kids – a 50/50 chance of pulling through. Even on March 10, when I left the Health Sciences Centre in Winnipeg, the doctor in charge of my care told Sue I was still a very sick man and "not out of the woods yet."

Another comment made by the same specialist was that because I was fit the clot hadn't killed me. He continued to say that the greatest danger I had been in was during the induced coma and there was a chance of organ failure. I had never thought that being physically fit was the best life insurance you can have. Now I know that being in shape gives you a fighting chance.

After I was allowed to go home, I still had to have bloodwork done every morning, visit my family doctor every afternoon and take numerous medications. I was also under the supervision of neuro-ophthalmologist Dr. Suresh Subramaniam at Rockyview Hospital in Calgary.

I was extremely limited in terms of what I could do. Until my vision began to improve, I was barely able to get around, let alone go running, swimming, driving or cycling. Eventually, I was able to start walking the pathway outside our home. I gradually got stronger and, on March 16, I began what I called the Long Walk to Recovery. I covered 3 kilometres and then had a nap.

By March 22 I was able to use my ski poles and walk for about 4 kilometres – Sue accompanied me, and it took us an hour and 15 minutes. Sue joked that at this pace I would be setting a new PB in no time. At this point in my recovery, the medications seemed to be taking effect and spinal fluid was no longer building up.

On March 27 Dr. Subramaniam showed us a scan of my brain, which clearly indicated complete blockage of the vein that extends down to my jugular. It seemed that nothing further had developed since the original scan, taken at Grace Hospital. Dr. Subramaniam was pleased with my progress and the improvement in my vision. Still, he said that it would probably take the best part of a year for my body to slowly absorb the clot and for my vision to return to normal.

My days were spent taking meds, walking, eating (a bit) and sleeping. I Googled "cerebral venous sinus thrombosis" (CVST) and was surprised to see that in December 2012 Hillary Clinton was diagnosed with the condition and has since made a full recovery. If Hillary could do it, I knew I could, too.

On April 1 I had an MRI at Rockyview Hospital, and on April 10 I hit the 100-kilometre mark on the Long Walk to Recovery. Things were slowly looking up, and Sue and I even planned to take a break in Banff. However, on the morning of our departure we got a call from England. Sue's dad Eric had suddenly passed away, due to an aneurism. Sue didn't want to leave me, but she had to go to England to be with her family. Distraught, she set me up with some frozen meals and a list of names to call for help.

Over the next three weeks, I talked to Sue every day and did my daily walk. I worked my way up to 8 kilometres per day and hit the 200-kilometre mark on April 25. When Sue returned in early May, she joined me on my daily routine, and over the next month I hit the 500-kilometre mark. Susan Parker, the principal at Elizabeth Barrett School in Cochrane, told me that the students had been walking and running "Martin's May Marathon," and they wanted me to join them for the final day of school.

The support I had received from the community had been amazing. Cards and messages wishing me well kept my spirits up, and I was looking forward to the day with the children.

At 8:30 a.m., on May 22, I joined hundreds of students from Elizabeth Barrett, Manachaban and Cochrane High schools. We walked around and around the soccer field, and the kids wished me well. When the bell rang at 9:15 a.m., and the students headed back to class, I waved to them and walked away. I realized that at that moment, I felt good.

I knew I would come back, and I would come back strong.

Afterword

"The human spirit is stronger than anything
that can happen to it."

— GEORGE C. SCOTT, actor

In 2014 the Scotiabank Calgary Marathon organization held a special race to mark 50 years of the event, a 50-kilometre ultra, which I ran. In 2015 I was only able to participate in their Goodlife Fitness 5-kilometre walk. But I was grateful that I was fit enough to do it. At noon, on Sunday, May 31, Sue and I made our way to the start line, where we met our "Walk Club": Elaine, Ally, Neil, Brian, Tom, Alyssa and Kurt. I'm always excited at the start of any race, and it was no different for this one. When the gun went off, we surged forward like a herd of turtles. Over the next hour we chatted to spectators, hung out with moms and dads pushing strollers, thanked volunteers and enjoyed the aid stations. It was one of the most relaxed and fun races I've ever done.

Two weeks later Sue and I lined up for our second race of the year, the Footstock 5-kilometre Walk in Cochrane. I had hit the 600-kilometre mark in the Long Walk to Recovery and was looking forward to the race. For this event Sue and I picked up the pace and completed the 5 kilometres in a respectable 51 minutes and 35 seconds. At the end of the walk, we were tucking into a pancake and bacon brunch when we heard our names announced. We had both come in second in our respective age groups.

Since the diagnosis in Winnipeg, my speaking career had been put on hold, but I knew the time had come to step back into the ring. Fred Hurdman from Raymond James Wealth Management had asked me to make a presentation to clients. I was pretty nervous but got a tremendous reception. Talking about the events that occurred in late February made me realize how lucky I was to have pulled through. I could have been in a place where a CT scan was not available, and my clot could have caused a fatal stroke.

This presentation marked the first time I had talked about my medical condition in public, and I became emotional when I saw Sue in the audience. At the end of the presentation, I left the stage and gave Sue a huge hug. I know it can be harder to be the support person than it is to be the one who is sick.

Week after week, Sue and I maintained our regime, up to 8 kilometres of walking per day, and by early July we had reached the 800-kilometre mark. These walks gave Sue and I time to talk and enjoy nature. We walked all over Cochrane and then headed out to Bragg Creek, Canmore and Calgary. On July 10 I went to see Dr. Subramaniam, and he showed me a scan that showed the swelling at the back of my eye had gone down and my eyesight was back to normal.

He told me that the clot had shrunk considerably, but it was not gone. He reduced my number of medications and scheduled another MRI for September. He noted that there was still no way to identify a cause for the clot and just advised me to stay hydrated in the hot weather. At the end of the appointment, he gave me some great news. I could start running, playing tennis, swimming and driving again. Sue mentioned that she had some chores lined up, but I didn't think we should rush things.

On July 18 I embarked on my first run in 146 days. I was apprehensive as I slowly jogged down the road and onto the river path. My legs felt heavy, and my breathing was laboured. After ten minutes, however, I found my rhythm, and as I ran along the mighty Bow I had a huge smile on my face. I completed the 5 kilometres in 33 minutes and 29 seconds and felt that I was back.

At the end of August, Sue and I finally took the break we needed in Waterton Lakes National Park in southwest Alberta. We stayed in a cabin near Beaver Mines, which formed in the early 1900s with the opening of a coal mine. At one time, Beaver Mines had over 1,500 residents, however, because of the requirement for steel (rail tracks) during the wars and a reduced need for coal, the mines eventually closed and residents dispersed. The last mine shut down in 1971. For the past 30 years, Beaver Mines has been considered a ghost town and has been featured in many books. These days the main features of the hamlet are a general store, pub and tennis court. Yes, tennis again! Every morning we were there, Sue and I played tennis before heading out to explore.

Smoke from forest fires in the U.S. hung in the air, but we visited the park anyway, and enjoyed lunch at the Prince of Wales Hotel.

In the afternoon we stepped aboard the historic M.V. *International* and cruised along the shoreline of beautiful Upper Waterton Lake, crossing the international border to Goat Haunt, Montana. It was definitely an eerie feeling as the boat plowed across the lake with the smoke-shrouded mountains all around us.

Throughout the fall I felt that my running was going well, so on October 24, I undertook my first serious race. Kirsten Fleming, race director of the Calgary Marathon, suggested I enter the 10-kilometre Dash of Doom. This is a fancy-dress event, and Kirsten thought I should dress up as a doctor, to show the clot who was boss. I liked the idea, and Sue and I came up with my alter ego, Captain Clot-Buster.

I lined up in my doctor's scrubs, a Canada buff with two eye holes and swimming goggles with the lenses removed. The race went well: I ran it in 51 minutes and 21 seconds. It was not only a personal best for Captain Clot-Buster but I also won second prize in the best-outfit category.

Two days later Sue showed me an article from the *Guardian* that would change the direction of my life. The story featured a female runner named Zainab. She had become the first Afghani woman to run a marathon, in the first ever Marathon of Afghanistan. In the article, Zainab talked about her training. "The children were stoning us, the people said bad words like 'prostitutes, why don't you stay at home? You are destroying Islam.'" It got me thinking.

We're so lucky to live where we do. Every weekend, we can sign up for a race and the only thing holding us back is our desire to participate. In some countries this is not the case, particularly for women. I had heard about the same kind of discrimination in Benin, West Africa, when Heather Moyse and Caroline Ouellette (RTP Athlete

Ambassadors) talked to the women's national soccer team. The team members said they were treated like outcasts and freaks.

After reading the article, I made a vow. If I could recover in time, I would run the 2016 Marathon of Afghanistan and support Zainab's efforts to show that sport is for everyone. When I told Sue, she said I could go as long as I took my family doctor with me. I immediately asked Bill Hanlon, and he said yes. Game on. In the following days, I contacted James Bingham, the race director, and James Wilcox from Untamed Borders, a trip organizer. The wheels were in motion.

With a renewed focus, my running continued to go well. However, I was having some difficulty with my level of endurance. Some of the runs were tough to finish, and I didn't have much motivation. I was looking for something to grab my imagination and propel me forward, and thanks to my friend Glenda, I found it. The Vert180 was a ski mountaineering event scheduled to take place at Canada Olympic Park (COP) on the evening of Saturday, December 5. The objective of this particular race was to complete as many loops as you could up and down the ski hill at Canada Olympic Park, in three hours. For extra practice before the race, I did a clinic with Kylee Toth Ohler, one of Canada's top "skimo" racers. For two hours, Kylee showed me how to attach skins to the skis, adjust the bindings for climbing uphill, remove the skins and ski down and strap the skis to a backpack for the March of Death section of the race.

The evening of the event was clear and –7°C. The hill was fully lit, and a group of 60 people lined up for the start. I had decided on my customary "slow and steady" approach, and when the gun went off, I let the majority of the group blaze ahead. I soon got into my stride, and we climbed the incline, one after the other, forming a snake of skiers. At the top, I stripped the skins off the skis, clicked the bindings into downhill mode and skied down. My quads were burning as I entered the finishing chute, and it was time to do it all over again. Over the next three hours, I completed eight loops, only nine behind the eventual winning man and woman, who did 17 each.

To further inspire myself, I tried my 60th sport: luge. It was my 60th birthday, and I felt up to the challenge. I found myself back at COP, lined up in the ice house with a group of 9- and 10-year-olds to get instructions. It was pretty straightforward: point your toes and keep your head down. I waited ten minutes to take my turn, and then I climbed the stairs, sat on the luge and away I went. Heading into the first curve, it climbed up the bank. Then I was shot out into a straightaway and then into another curve. Before I knew it, the ride was over, and I was slowing up in the finish chute. It was exhilarating. I felt ready to tackle anything.

Before I could contemplate the next sport I wanted to try – pickleball – Sue and I had Calum over for Christmas. At first, he wasn't sure if he should come because Sue's mom, Terryanne, had just recently gone to the hospital, not feeling well. However, her condition didn't appear to be critical, so he decided to make the trip.

On December 23, a day after Calum arrived, Lynne called to say that Terryanne had passed away.

Terryanne championed everything I did – she called me her "Brit with Grit." Since Sue's dad had passed away in April, she had moved into a care home. She was a talented poet. I still love reading her poetry, and the following is one of my favourites:

The Winner

Mane blown back on straining neck,
Eyes alight and nostrils wide,
Gallant steed, in gallop set,
Breathing hard with every stride.

Muscles taut with glistening sweat,
Thundering flight to vibrant ground,
Hooves and sinew meeting yet,
Limbs of steel, on new turf pound.

Spittled mouth, with swollen tongue,
Rushing blood, heart fit to burst,
Fiery surge to shatter lung,
Duty-bound to come in first.

It had been a really tough year for Sue, having to deal with the shock of my illness and losing both of her parents, all within a matter of months. Christmas was a sad time for us all. In early January, she and Calum travelled back to England for Terryanne's funeral.

On December 31, before they left, we all took part in the Sixth Annual Marathon Quest 250 Run/Walk, this time to raise $10,000 for a kindergarten playground in Mto wa Mbu, Tanzania. With a total of 116 runners, we raised $4,970. Adding this to the amount raised online brought us up to $12,066. The kindergarten kids of Mto wa Mbu would get a playground, bouncy castle and some books to start a library.

And I was thrilled to have completed my first and last marathon of 2015 in 5 hours, 16 minutes and 1 second.

In late February 2016 I returned to Winnipeg. Susanne, organizer of the Recreation Connections Manitoba conference, asked me to go back and finish what I had started, before my clot put the brakes on my speaking at her event. It was quite emotional, seeing her and Cory again and standing on the main stage of the Metropolitan Entertainment Centre in front of 300 people. An hour later I received a standing ovation, and I was completely overwhelmed.

In mid-April I had some good news about the clot. I went to see my specialist and he said that it had reduced by 95 per cent. He wanted me to have another CT scan in July and then he would decide whether or not he could take me off all my medications.

My training had gone well for the Calgary Marathon, and at 7 a.m., on May 29, 2016, the gun went off and Captain Clot-Buster started his first official marathon race. It was a warm day and all along the route people were shouting out their support. Sometimes they weren't quite sure who I was: "Go Captain America," "You're almost there, Canada Man," and "You're looking good, Captain Blood-Clot" were some of the words of encouragement. Still, it didn't matter what they shouted out, it all helped me to finish in 4 hours, 24 minutes and 40 seconds.

I am a member of the Canadian Association of Professional Speakers and at the monthly meeting in mid-March I got into a conversation with Kate McKenzie who, for seven years, had been a junior high school teacher and is now an author, artist and documentary filmmaker. She had read *Marathon Quest* and was wondering what I had next on the horizon. I told her about the Marathon of Afghanistan. Kate was hooked. We had further conversations and plans started to develop to film a documentary of the race. Kate's cousin Scott Townend is also a documentary filmmaker. He lives in Edmonton and, in early June, we all met up at Kate's place to shoot the trailer. The storyline is that I am training Kate to run her first marathon, and it will be in Afghanistan. In early July, the trailer, or "sizzle reel," for the documentary was completed. It was now time to get funding for the film.

As I write this, in August 2016, Sue and I are planning a short holiday to Penticton, BC, in early September. This time our accommodation will not be a tent, a B & B or a hotel but a VW Westphalia camper van. In the late 1960s and early 70s, Mum and Dad took me and my two brothers and three sisters across Europe in one of these iconic vehicles. I like camping, but Sue doesn't like sleeping on the ground so the van will be perfect for both of us.

Once we're back, we'll focus on the trip to Afghanistan. I'm a little apprehensive, as every day there seems to be more bad news from that part of the world. However, I know there are people over there trying to make a difference. They want a better life for themselves and their children. I, too, want a world where all children can strive to achieve their dreams in an environment free of ridicule and abuse. I also know that this won't happen unless action is taken.

So it's up to all of us. In life you don't have to do a lot, but you have to do something!

Acknowledgements

This journey could not have been undertaken without the help of many individuals, groups and organizations. The ongoing support of Right To Play Canada, particularly Sarah Stern and Johann Koss, has proved invaluable. Seeing the work they do with children inspired me to undertake Quests for Kids. The information I include in this book about Right To Play and PLAY programs, and quotations related to those programs and their leaders, are sourced from Right To Play and PLAY year-in-review publications.

Each quest involved many people giving their time and effort. In Netball Quest, it was Julie Arnold and Netball Alberta Association; in Lacrosse Quest, Scott and Shawn Cable and their company, Hot Box Lacrosse, as well as Geoff Snider and Andrew McBride of the Calgary Roughnecks. Jason Webb, owner of Downunder Travel, organized Cook Island Quest, and Lucy Lovelock of the Cochrane Rangers pulled together the teams and volunteers for Soccer Quest, while Robin Mitchell provided the venue at Spray Lake Sawmills Family Sports Centre.

Hockey Quest succeeded due to the efforts of Kelly and Reid Kimmett, Jason Baserman and Joe MacLellan; and Kilimanjaro Quest would not have happened without Lau and Leesha Mafuru of Boma Africa. Aaron McConnell, co-owner of TransRockies, sponsored my participation in TransRockies Quest. Rotarians Stephen Lay and David Laud, members of the many participating Rotary clubs and Right To Play UK, made Rotary Coastal Quest a reality. Alex Baum, at Cochrane Toyota, provided the Tacoma Questmobile for Canada Quest for Kids; Peter and Gabe donated the Quest buffs and McDonald's the food. A huge thanks to the Right To Play clubs of the universities of Quest, Calgary, Alberta, Western, Wilfrid Laurier, Toronto, Ryerson, Humber, McGill, New Brunswick, Mount Allison and Memorial that found the players and volunteers.

Others that have contributed over the years include 4iiii Innovations, Abony Family Tennis Centre, Back on Track, the *Cochrane Times* and *Cochrane Eagle*, Ink'd Graphics, Garmin, Pat's Palette Pleasers and the Redwood Meadows Right To Play Team. The Rotary Club of Cochrane, Kirsten Flemming at the Scotiabank Calgary Marathon Association and Elaine Kusper at IMPACT magazine have provided support and guidance throughout.

After the quests, I fought and won my biggest challenge with help from Cory Jackson and Susanne Moore of Recreation Connections Manitoba, staff at the Grace and Health Science Centre in Winnipeg, my family doctor Bill Hanlon and neuro-ophthalmologist Dr. Subramaniam at Rockyview General Hospital in Calgary.

A special mention goes to our dear friends John and Jo-Anne Wilson, Wayne and Cathy Benz, Tom and Ulrica Healy, and Sue's sister, Lynne, for their unending and unconditional support throughout this whole journey, both during the quests and during my illness. Thank you.

This book and my previous one, *Marathon Quest*, would never have seen the light of day if it had not been for the backing and endless hours of hard work and support provided by Don Gorman and Rick Wood at Rocky Mountain Books and by my long-suffering, ever-positive editor, Meaghan Craven.

Thank you to our children, Kyle, Calum and Kristina, who encouraged me when the going got tough, and grandchildren Autumn, Nathan and Matthew Conner, who were my inspiration along the way. I love you guys very much.

Finally, Sue has been with me from the start, throughout my highs and lows, and always has faith that I can get the job done. I couldn't have done it without your love and support. I love you.

About the Author

At 47, Martin Parnell wasn't in shape for running. Thirteen years later he completed 250 marathons in one year and wrote about it in his award-winning book, *Marathon Quest*. He went on to set five Guinness World Records in endurance events, summited Mount Kilimanjaro in 21 hours and ran 1000 kilometres along the South West Coastal Path of England in 25 days. These activities were all part of his Quest for Kids initiative: ten quests in five years that raised $1.36 million for the humanitarian organization Right To Play. His fundraising activities helped change the lives of over 27,000 children.

During his 25-year career in the Canadian mining industry, Martin worked in various capacities in engineering, operations and human resources. Martin has written for *Huffington Post* and various other local, national and international publications. He was awarded the Queen Elizabeth II Diamond Jubilee Medal and was named one of the *Calgary Herald*'s "20 Compelling Calgarians."

Today, Martin is an international keynote speaker, workshop leader and consultant. He is also an elite endurance athlete and philanthropist.

Martin is a member of the Rotary Club of Cochrane, Alberta, where he lives with his wife, Sue. They have three children, Kyle, Calum and Kristina, and three grandchildren, Autumn, Nathan and Matthew Connor. Sue and Martin enjoy walking, snowshoeing and tennis. Martin can often be seen running the pathways along the Bow River, near their home.

Visit www.martinparnell.com,
contact Martin at info@martinparnell.com
or call him by dialling 403-668-1669.